THE POWER OF BRAND ENGAGEMENT

GAURAV GULATI

Copyright © 2018 Gaurav Gulati

All rights reserved.

ISBN: 978-93-5311-111-3

All rights reserved. No part of this publication may be reproduced, distributed, or transmitted in any form or by any means, including photocopying, recording, or other electronic or mechanical methods, without the prior written permission of the author, except in the case of brief quotations embodied in critical reviews and certain other noncommercial uses permitted by copyright law. For permission requests, write to the author, addressed "Attention: Permissions Coordinator," at the address below.

Email: info@gauravgulati.com
Web: www.gauravgulati.com

THANK YOU

Dear Lord,

Every time I complete my book, I am surprised! I don't know why but it becomes difficult to believe that I wrote one more book. I know, I can never complete and publish the book without your blessings. I get astonished when new and fresh ideas come in front of me automatically, and I get more and more meaningful content to write.

Thank you so much for caring about me, guiding me and forgiving me countless time.

ACKNOWLEDGMENTS

I could never have done this without faith and support of my father Ripu Daman Gulati and mother Kamini Gulati. Thank you for teaching me to believe in myself, in God and my dreams.

Special thanks to my wife Ritika Gulati for always standing by me in the most trying time and telling me each time 'Don't Worry Everything Will Be Alright.'

PREFACE

Winning customers is a concept that brands aspire for. When you win customers, they don't just buy your products or avail your services; your bond with them is not fleeting or seasonal. It is worth the time and effort that you invest to nurture such a bond. They think of your brand first when they are in need. They seek you out even when there are other brands, more popular and newer, that compete for their precious attention. The best practices of Brand Engagement give you this irresistible influence to your customers.

This book provides insights to winning brand engagement strategies that captivate people and conquer their hearts. It talks about the value of engaging with your customers to the relevance and longevity of your brand.

Are you dreaming of the success of your brand or business? The pages of this book will show you the best course of action if you want to realize your dream. It is filled with practical, creative and up-to-date tips that you can use to foster a long-lasting connection with your customers. The key is authenticity. Your brand should showcase endearing qualities that people resonate with. Relationships between brands and customers should happen organically.

These strategies are not just concepts. They are examples that you can incorporate into your business today. They are straightforward and relevant to an offline and online brand. The principles of brand engagement are universally applicable, and they tackle everyday issues that entrepreneurs can often ignore. With the informative and helpful approach of this book, you are bound to find creative ways to apply the strategies in an organized and efficient system sooner.

GAURAV GULATI

ABOUT THE AUTHOR

Gaurav Gulati understands that in life, as in business, visibility is everything. As a personal branding & brand engagement consultant, he pushes boundaries and challenges limitations!

We're living in a tech-driven, interconnected world where personal brand and brand engagement go hand-in-hand. That's why he's dedicated himself to provide individuals and businesses with the strategies to future-proof their brands and boost engagement in this artificial intelligence world.

Gulati's signature brand building and brand engagement system encourages each client, from artists and models to entrepreneurs and politicians, to harness the power of their personal brand so they can work smarter, stretch farther and transform into thriving profitable monoliths. His innovative approach has been featured in various media reports and blogs and earned him the title of Asia's Leading Personal Branding & Engagement Consultant.

Gaurav Gulati holds an MBA in Marketing, PGD in International Management from University of the West of England and a BBA.HM. He has also studied Brand Management from the University of London and Personal Branding from the University of Virginia. As a Certified Six Sigma Black Belt Professional and Project Management Professional, he's got a unique insight into cross-industry trends and the cutting edge of brand positioning. Gulati's innovative approach is founded on the idea that in our fast-paced, increasingly digital age, everybody we meet has the potential to be a powerhouse influencer.

As a life observer, he regularly writes on business practices, management, brands and branding. His writing highlights real strategies to motivate and inspire.

GAURAV GULATI

THE POWER OF BRAND ENGAGEMENT

INTRODUCTION	XIII
1. UNDERSTANDING BRANDS	15
2. CREATING A SUCCESSFUL BRAND	25
3. DELVING DEEPER INTO BRAND ENGAGEMENT	37
4. BENEFITS OF CONNECTING WITH CUSTOMERS	47
5. STRATEGIES THAT CONQUER CONSUMER'S HEARTS	55
6. WINNING BRAND ENGAGEMENT	63
7. STRATEGIES THAT BOOST BRAND ENGAGEMENT	69
8. NEGATIVE BRAND ENGAGEMENT	77
9. WHY PERSONAL BRANDING MATTERS?	87
10. IMPACT AND INFLUENCE OF CULTURE	93
11. HUMANIST BRANDING	99
12. NETWORKING	105

GAURAV GULATI

INTRODUCTION

In the world of traditional and modern businesses – online and offline – customers and clients have a special role to play. They are not just part of the target market. They are human beings with thoughts and emotions which brands should recognize and respect.

Brand engagement is a conversation with our customers and clients. Considered a two-way street, it is a significant connection between a brand and the people it aims to reach. Through our branding efforts, we can reach out to them in a memorable and meaningful way. We establish a relationship that they can trust and benefit from. Both parties, the brands and the customers, should be in a win-win situation all the time.

Some companies or businesses think that it's enough to put their products out there and hire an advertising team to deal with the customer engagement aspect but they realize in the end that they are mistaken. They lose money, miss lucrative opportunities and fail in their marketing initiatives because they are complacent. You don't have to make the same mistakes. In these modern times, there are several strategies and methods that work which will be shown to you in this valuable book.

Real brand engagement, the one that appeals to customers in a rational and emotional level, is hard to achieve but it's not impossible. You just have to be mindful of your next course of action. Don't believe in marketing trends that have not proven great results for the long-term. It takes time to engage in a sincere exchange of ideas with your customers. You have to listen to what they want and be keen in observing what kind of engagement they respond warmly to. Are you ready to share a unique experience with your customers and clients?

Read the pages of this book and learn how meaningful brand engagement can be effective in establishing and cultivating a long-term professional relationship with your customers. Interact with them in a way that they can see the value of your brand to their lives. Watch as your brand thrives in sales and profits while you bask in the light of your customers' attention, loyalty and love.

1

UNDERSTANDING BRANDS

The phrase "Brand" can easily be explained as a word commonly used in distinguishing an item or entity from others. It is also used in indicating ownership of a particular property, e.g., products and services of a company. The brand can even go to the extent of letting you know the degree of quality of service or product a company offers. You know people in the past too had belongings such as cows, sheep, horses, human slaves as well as so many other things. You may be wondering how come they were able to distinguish their belonging from another; branding made that possible, and this is as a result of a label, name or mark that has been impressed on those so-called belongings for ease of identification.

It is essential to note that the term 'Brand' can be viewed differently from the angle of a business owner and end-users. Business always consider Brand as an instrument of distinguishing their various goods and services apart from that of other business' while the end-users see it as means of identifying the quality of particular goods and services offered by a business.

The term branding comes from the Old Norse "Brand" which means to burn. Cattle, slaves, timber and earthenware were burnt or branded with the markings or symbols of the owner using a hot iron rod. The idea of branding was basically to represent ownership, in precise things which had value.

DISTINGUISHING BRAND FROM BRANDING

A brand can be referred to the identity of any business in respect of the goods and services offered by a business. It can as well be a name, symbol or combination of the name and logo in identifying the products or services of the business entity. However, branding is the process involved in creating a brand or brands and managing it towards consumer satisfaction.

Your business's brand is the overall impression you present to customers. A brand is developed using a combination of what your establishment really does or creates, with supporting elements like language, visual components, and other aesthetic components.

Parts of your brand include:

- What you do
- What you offer
- How you define yourself (through written content, marketing materials etc.)
- Visual elements like Logo, Photos, Videos, Colour Schemes, Fonts etc.

Some of these, particularly the visual elements, can appear insignificant to someone who isn't aware with how a brand is developed and how even the tiniest parts of what a company presents to the audience help contribute to the overall way they're perceived. Which colours you pick, what fonts appear in your written materials and website, and how your logo looks can make a remarkable difference in what energy your public presence puts off; which can produce a meaningful impact on the success of your company.

Branding is the process of creating the brand, positioning your business, making choices that support your brand goal, and applying the various components throughout your company that achieve that goal. The process, when done accurately, should be a reasonably time-consuming thing.

FEATURES OF BRAND

Passion

It is certainly impossible to build a brand without passion; you can create a business without passion but not a brand. When you study about really successful people like Steve Jobs or Bill Gates, you will learn they all had a serious passion that keeps driving them to work hard and constantly deliver greatness. That energy leads to enthusiasm and authentic joy, which is irresistible. Passion is the root to success because it fuel confidence, creates excitement and is contagious.

Clarity

Clarity is a must, in having a real and acceptable brand. A brand must indicate precisely who you are, what you offer, what you stand for, the outcome you are aiming for, as well as the quality or your product and services. Your brand must be able to represent all these clearly for acceptability. However, there are still numerous features of brand apart from those mentioned above which includes competitiveness, awareness, acceptability to mention a few.

Uniqueness

When establishing a brand, it merely means you are setting your products or services apart from those that are available in a particular region, through the physical appearance or quality of a product as well as the level of efficiency offered through a service. Uniqueness is the most effective brand shortcut to attract customers. Some benefits of uniqueness are as below:

- Attention: Attracts the buyer's attention
- Quicker: Gets in the buyer's brain faster
- Recall: Is much remembered
- Favouring: Gives the buyer good reasons to choose your brand
- Reduce Competition: Narrows the competition - enabling you to develop better products, charge higher prices, and make more profits.

Consistency

Consistency is a major feature when it comes to brand or branding; this is because it goes a long way in the management of views, signifies professionalism, reliability, purpose, and stability. It also explains a business's mindset, eradicates concerns surrounding brand confusion, safeguards investment and builds upon past accomplishments.

Loyalty

Brand loyalty can be referred to as brand integrity and is of the most vital feature. Brand loyalists' customers buy particular brand products irrespective of the situation. Many consumers prefer using specific brands goods regardless of many other types available, all because of the unique benefits derived from the product. However, the suitable approach to developing brand loyalty is always to stay in close contact with consumers coupled with sustaining a higher level of customer satisfaction.

BENEFITS OF AN EFFECTIVE BRAND

An effective brand;

- enhances business goodwill and the profitability
- influences consumer's decision on whether to buy or not
- can easily rise the price and still experience an increase in demand
- can result in creating and maintaining customers trust in a product or service
- can save a business irrespective of any adverse situation it might be experiencing
- makes a product/ service outstanding and easily distinguished from other brands
- helps to enhance market share as a result of the brand acceptance by the end-users
- gives room for a friendly relationship among users of the same brand which can further lead to the creation of the brand's awareness for higher turnover
- signifies to consumers that you are ready and determined to meet their needs for a long time to come

Nowadays individuals do not only buy because of the benefits of a product or service but also because of the psychological and emotional attachment to the brand. Furthermore, a strong brand possesses some characteristics that some tagged as the 3Cs.

Clarity: Brand clarity means nothing else than that your brand works as a whole. A strong brand must be clear of any misconception surrounding it. It must also have a definite value that can distinguish it from that of other competing brands in the target market.

Constancy: Constancy means showing through everything you do that you are dependable. A strong brand is that which delivers expected quality and quantity of product or services to end-users irrespective of any situation. Dependability is another bedrock of trust.

Consistency: This goes back to promise. A strong brand is consistent in everything, and this is one of the elements that sustain them. Bruce Springsteen said. "It demands a consistency of thought, of purpose, and of action over a long period of time." He was speaking about his journey to music stardom, yet his statements are just as applicable to the world of brands.

WHY BRANDS MATTER IN EVERY BUYING DECISION OF THE CONSUMER

To demonstrate how brands have used their cohesive quality of influencing the consumer with their purchase choices is not just about price as we read it in economics. Well, the price is an important aspect that helps a brand run the competition, but on a bigger view, various other factors such as logo, design, description, personality, service, safety and background come in action before any product or service can be bought.

The primary wants of an average customer are a comfort, happiness and satisfaction. If a brand succeeds to deliver all of these necessities to the consumer, then the customer builds a strong opinion about the brand and makes it the primary source of its particular needs.

Brand Loyalty

Now imagine you have just entered the grocery store in search of coffee, which shelf could you go first? There are at least ten brands that sell coffee powder at nearly the same price, but you buy one particular brand, you had made up your mind even before you entered the store, that phenomenon is called brand loyalty.

Brand Loyalty is the milder form of "Brand Evangelism" and gives the customer tendencies to continue buying goods of the same brand instead of various available choices. This 'Will' and 'Choice' is not a result of the customer's ignorance, but it influenced through the brand's differentiation from its competitors. Brands that aim for becoming market leaders always introduce comprehensive strategies in their marketing mix to win their niche. By offering precisely what the consumer is looking for is the secret of creating loyal customers.

Brands Help in Decision Making

Another reason to invest in brand loyalty drives is now more crucial than ever. When a customer is looking to buy a new mobile, he opens Amazon App on his mobile and search mobiles. What he gets is hundreds of search results. This puts the customer in a quite complicated situation and the result - customer loses interest and quits. But, what if he types 'iPhone' in the search box and gets 10-15 results? Now that's manageable figure from which the consumer can promptly narrow down his choices. Brand loyalty is not only about making profits, but also giving consumers a source to always trust. Once the trust has been established, the shopper no longer needs to browse hundreds of searches or hundreds of shelves.

Brands Produce Memories

Even though brands represent inanimate products and lifeless systems but they perform enough responsiveness when you communicate with them. Products and Services share those moments that define the beginning of relationship about to be set in stone. You must have had that memory when your energy drink gave you the required energy during your exam when you needed it most. Or that one perfect brake you made that saved you from an unfortunate car accident. The products you have tried leave a memory, and that is what keeps you buying them, again and again, no matter what.

Brands Offer Sense of Security

Have you ever purchased a product and been offered a peace-of-mind guarantee or a peace-of-mind protection plan? Another great thing about buying from a reliable brand is the security and safety it offers. When you purchase a cell phone from a particular brand you always buy from; you will rest assured that your decision is perfect because of quality and performance the product offers every time. You have peace of mind, and this means you trust the cell phone's display screen, operating system, sound quality and battery life. But most importantly, the money you paid will be worth what you get.

Brands Add Value

Choosing between brands is not about selecting the shiniest product, it's about the total value that motivates the consumer's mind. In this competitive world where more than one brand is producing the same product with almost same features, the buyer is likely to buy the one which puts him in a higher position in the society. From laundry detergents to clothes and gadgets to vehicles, the brand you wear, use or drive is a reflection of who you are and where you fit. A Brand logo on your products, clothes or car is the status advocate you who speaks about your status.

Brand Evangelism

Brand evangelism is the extreme form of brand loyalty, and it exists quite lots among consumer groups. From iPhone and Oneplus, Coke and Pepsi, Nike and Reebok to Hyundai and Suzuki, every brand that sells cell phones, beverages, footwear or cars are in competition. Similarly, brand evangelists are always in competition, commenting and showing off the perfection of one brand from the other. Various studies show that each brand evangelist, on average, creates about three new customers. So, if you're able to build up a clientele of 10 brand evangelists, you could easily be looking at 30 new customers.

Conclusion: It doesn't matter if you are a big or small business selling cars or small furniture, brand building is essential, and brand driven marketing is the best angle for selling your products and services for business growth.

GAURAV GULATI

2

CREATING A SUCCESSFUL BRAND

Brands outlive products. Brands promise consistency, reliability and experience. Brands are valuable; many businesses put the value of their brand on their balance sheet. Successful brand building process surpasses the competition and plays a vital role to create brand engagement. You need to build a strong bond with your customer to make your brand successful. Brand building is a continuous process which determines your company's vision and position in the market.

A successful brand building process drives engagement and advocates your product or service. As a business, you must be ready to keep track on brand strategies used by your competitors; this helps you to re-strategize and be one step ahead. Most people think the brand is all about "the logo," but a logo is just the beginning of a brand's visual aspect which also includes the website, marketing materials, taglines, press releases, and advertisements etc. A brand is so much more than a logo or its visual elements, and building a strong brand represents your company's true spirit.

PROCESS IN CREATING A STRONG BRAND

Offer Quality Products and Services

Beginning a business' brand journey with quality product and service provides a reliable platform for brand acceptability in the market. And apart from the brand's acceptance in the market, lot more efforts need to be put into the process of sustaining, so it does not experience any form of reductions in the demand for the brand.

Manage your Brand Effectively

To manage your brand means you will need to identify the core uniqueness of the brand, specify your objectives clearly and also give the brand a perfect placing in the target market. As stated earlier, keep a close eye on the competition. There is an old saying, "What you don't know won't hurt you." No! That's Not True! It can, and it will hurt you. It's important to know as much as you can about your market, your customers, your products, your services and your competition.

Use of the Right Tagline or Phrase

There is no doubt that taglines are essential for business even to the extent that their taglines recognize some brands and the tagline profoundly influences their standing in the market. Therefore, no matter how big or small your business is, what you must have is a perfect tagline. For example; Nike uses "Just Do It", "The Real Thing" for Coke, "Safe" for Volvo, and so on.

Emotional Utilization

That should be no surprise; studies show that people rely on emotions more than information to make brand decisions. Emotional dimensions clearly separate businesses from their competitors and help to generate engagement.

Image Building

The brand image is critical, as it is an accumulation of feelings and opinions about that particular brand. Image of a brand is a deciding factor that determines the sales. In building the image of a brand, you also need focus on superficial elements such as the name, logo and design as this helps in passing out the relevant message to the consumer and better the chances of the brand acceptability.

Brand Personality

Brand personality is defined as the set of human characteristics that are associated with a brand. The way a brand behaves or expresses itself is what Brand personality is all about. In addition to its functional benefits, brand personality is a quantifying value-add to your brand. The framework of brand personality helps businesses to pave the way its customers would feel about its product or services. As we humans showcase a varied range of behavioral attributes such as caring, fun, anger, rebel etc., so does the brand for our business would while communicating with its consumers. Jennifer Aaker, General Atlantic professor of marketing at the Graduate School of business in her study identified core brand personality dimensions which are a combination of above set of adjectives. Under her study, the five core dimensions of brand personality are Sincerity, Excitement, Competence, Sophistication and Ruggedness.

Brand Design

It takes a thoughtfully designed strategy to improve communication and environments that define, inspire and engage consumers. For a phrase or word to be outstanding on a page, it needs to be stylishly formatted. It enhances identification and gives additional meaning to wordings. Brand Logo comprises of colours, diagrams, and lettering, to showcase the kind of value offered by the brand.

The logo of a brand is a physical component that is one of the biggest asset of the business. Every single brand has its separate logo; however, irrespective of the numerous companies with the various brand in a target market, they all have different and distinct logo designs for their brands.

Mojo Features:

Text Brand Name: No matter how small, a business must represent itself or its brand with a name or combination of letters for identification, e.g. Coke, Dell, Lenovo etc.

Shapes: This enhances the attraction of a brand logo. It can be in the form of a circle, square, triangle, diagrams or their combination to form suitable design for the brand.

Fonts: It is common to see lettering on or with brand logo having different fonts of style which beautifies the logo the more.

Colours: These are carefully selected to represent what a brand stands for and for a natural attraction of prospective users. E.g. Google having different colours for the letters in the name.

Colour Associations: Once you know your brand personality, you can start explaining it with colours. To do so, you have to understand the basics of colour psychology and what particular colour represents:

- White- Purity
- Black- Luxury
- Purple- Royalty
- Green- Health and environment
- Red – Excitement, energy, courage
- Blue- Tranquility, and peace
- Yellow- Cheerfulness, Relaxation, and lightness

BRAND NAMES

A brand name gives a business identity such as HP, Dell, Toyota, and Honda, etc. With a brand name, a product or service can easily be identified, and in some cases, a brand name signifies the degree of quality offered through any product. However, the process of choosing brand names should not be taken lightly, as a 'not too' suitable name can put some individual off a product.

You may be thinking what makes up a good brand name? Some features of good brand names are as below:

- It must be able to attract attention to the brand
- It must be simple; for easy remembrance and pronunciation
- A brand name must indeed be a meaningful or creative

- In addition to creating awareness, must be able to create a positive picture
- It must create certain emotions that will compel consumers to purchase the brand

Major benefit of brand names:

- Prevents products mix-up
- Convenient brand identification by customers
- It hints the prospective consumer about a brand
- Give additional advantage in a competitive environment
- It drives engagement and enhances customer loyalty
- It makes the introduction of new product easily distinguished in a target market

TYPES OF BRAND NAMES

Descriptive Names

Descriptive names are those that freely suggest the service or product offered by a company. Because of this, they tend to be unexceptional. While functional and practical, descriptive names leave little room for creativity on the part of the brand. These kinds of names are difficult to trademark. E.g. General Motors, Cartoon Network, The Weather Chanel, Hotel.com etc.

Suggestive Names

Suggestive names are evocative, creative and extraordinary as they make a significant differentiation. They're usually the cornerstone of a brand's positioning as they tell the consumer something about the product or service. These kinds of names are simple to trademark. E.g. Pepsi, Pampers, Digene etc.

Freestanding Names

The idea of freestanding names is quite simple; the best part is that you always create it the way you like it and the actual words have nothing to do with company activity. Are mostly based on founder or material or geographical names. E.g. Pringles, Old Spice, Gillette, Dell, Marks & Spencer, New York Life etc.

BRAND EXTENSION

Brand extension happens when one of your flagship brands ventures into a new market. To most marketers, brand extensions are accustomed occurrences. Likewise, businesses also have a convenient way of accessing new market or region via brand extension; hence, the extension of a brand is the process of creating a new business or product line as well as improving the existing ones through a strategic process.

TYPES OF BRAND EXTENSION

Product-Related Brand Extension: This type of expansion is commonly known as the line extension, and it is made from a line of already existing product. E.g., Pepsi drink resulting in an extension of other various types of drink that can still be associated with Pepsi- Pepsi Snacks.

Image-Related Brand Extension: This type of extension is those that possess some reasonable connection to the primary or existing brand. For instance, Reebok going into sports equipment and certification.

Unrelated Brand Extension: This extension is entirely

different from the one mentioned above in the sense that it is not similar to the existing brand in any way. For example, TATA brand name appearing on steel, cars, mobile network, to mention a few.

BENEFITS OF BRAND EXTENSION:

- Adding more shelf space e.g. Gillette Shaving Foams variants
- Developing a better version of an existing brand, e.g. Tide Plus – Remove stains better
- Widening the scope of customer's expectation, e.g. Waterproof Band-Aid
- Understanding market condition, e.g. Colgate Sensitive or Colgate Whitening
- Making more product alternative available to customers, e.g. Colgate have different types of products

Businesses majorly makes decision to extend beyond their existing products/services for many different motives; and some of which are:

- Adding varieties for better satisfaction
- Business maximizing its capacity to increasingly meet consumer's needs
- Creating some excitement around an old brand for better performance
- Widening the scope of the benefits of a product/service to new consumers
- Putting under control changes that might occur in the target market

- The core reason for extension is also to satisfy the need of unsatisfied end-users
- To better meet the ever-increasing needs of consumers
- To cover more regions in the target market
- For increase revenue and profitability

Developing Sub-Brands

The moment market competition increases or engagement drops, brand marketers also strive to widen the scope covered by the extension of both related and unrelated product or service groups. There is this typical mentality that the image, trust as well as the goodwill of a brand often rubs on the new category of extension thereby creating a sound platform for widespread awareness and swift acceptability. There are well-known brands that have consistently made use of expansion within the similar category and have achieved tremendous success. For example; Unilever's sub-brands are Dove, Sunsilk, Lux and Suave.

Dual Branding

Dual branding also known as co-branding can be defined as a partnership between two or more brands for products and services. It also happens to be the combined arrangement between two brands to come up with a new brand or products or services that possess the features of the two brands involved. Such partnership is an effective method to expand business operation through improved brand engagement that can drive into a new market. The aim of co-branding is for the two separate brands to compliment themselves through their high points for better engagement, acceptability and profitability.

TYPES OF CO-BRANDING

Same Business Co-Branding: This is when different products within the same business are co-branding. E.g. Colgate Tooth Paste and Tooth Brush

Multiple Co-Branding: This is when more than two brand comes together to co-brand their products together. E.g. Citibank with British Airways

Ingredient Co-Branding: This is when a well-known brand is co-brand with an upcoming brand; this partnership is to showcase the forthcoming brand for full acceptability in the market. This type of branding occurs regularly within a business to boost the engagement of their new product or service. E.g. Pillsbury Brownies with Nestle Chocolate

Composite Co-branding: This refers to the use of two notable brand names in a way that they can collectively offer a distinguished product/service that could not be possible individually. E.g. Dell with Intel

CORPORATE BRANDING

Corporate branding is the practice of promoting the brand name of a business entity, as opposed to particular products or services. Irrespective of the fact that this type of branding only focuses on a business' name or image, it can still be carried out alongside co-branding.

Why corporate branding is vital for brand engagement?

There are numerous reasons why branding is so essential to both large and small companies, below are few reasons why branding is so important for business:

Identity: Corporate branding gives the business an identity. Your tagline and logo become the face of your business, which is why a strong establishment brand can be recognized by anyone even if the name of the company isn't visible.

Value: Corporate branding add value to your business, it creates value for both your existing customers as well as for potential customers. If you choose to sell the company in years to come, you could improve both value and salability with strong branding. Many businesses have made millions and billions because of good branding.

Trust: Most consumers only buy products from certain companies because their brand is one that they know and trust. Branding inevitably develops confidence that has the great impact on the success of business both in the short-term and the long-term.

GAURAV GULATI

3

DELVING DEEPER INTO BRAND ENGAGEMENT

Building a connection with your customers that is so close you can almost read their minds is an ability some gifted entrepreneurs have, but this is not exclusive to them. You can discover this great capacity in yourself and incorporate it into your business. A well-engaged brand is an entity that knows how to move forward. It is informed by the insights that it has gained straight from its customers. Knowing your customer is critical to any brand endeavor. Successful entrepreneurs know what their consumers want and the most potent way of making their goods or service available.

I can ask you to share information with your customers, and you may be willing to do that as a brand, a company or a business entity. But through this effort, do you think you are connecting with them? The answer is not yet. You have to wait for their response and evaluate the feedback. This exchange goes back and forth until you can correctly engage with your customers.

DEFINATION OF BRAND ENGAGEMENT

Brand engagement is an essential strategy to connect with your customers through rational and emotional communication. When brands go beyond showing their products and services, they engage with people through interactive marketing, storytelling and holistic experiences. They put their hearts out by sharing their brand philosophy and organizing events that allow customers to feel and experience what the brand has to offer. The customers' positive response and patronage becomes a natural outcome, not forced or manipulated, but willingly provided. This mutual brand and customer relationship translate to higher sales and increase in profits.

Real Brand Connection

Do you have an existing brand? Or, are you creating a new brand? Whether you're just starting out or needing an upgrade, you can't go wrong with establishing a strong brand engagement with your customers. Your connection with them should be authentic and sincere. This is particularly helpful for people who have service-oriented brands, and we know every brand is service-oriented now. You can't be rude to your customers when you own a hair salon or a daycare center for children or any other nature of the business. It's important that you talk to your customers in an amiable and friendly way in order to establish rapport and trust. Now, you have to create the character of your brand. Is your brand approachable and interactive? Or is it elitist and unreachable to a particular demographic? You can't please everybody so you have to stick to a list of qualities that you, your staff and your marketing team can adapt, replicate and project to the world.

An organic brand engagement should be deeply rooted in your

philosophy as a brand. What do you stand for? If your business strategy is to advocate environmental awareness through your products, then you have to create ads, infographics or marketing videos that share this message. Whether your business is offline or online, you can innovate ways to engage with your target market so that they can learn more about you and gravitate to your message.

If you choose the digital route, you can share thoughtful Facebook/Instagram (social media) posts that give your customers a glimpse into the character of your brand. For a physical store that sells fabrics, give your customers a chance to talk to a consultant to help them choose suitable fabrics for their homes. The people you interact with can express their likes and dislikes which become the valuable feedback that you can use to improve your brand. Successful brands make customers feel that they have a meaningful personal connection through experiences in stores and their online platforms.

Successfully Engage Offline

It's true that brand engagement online has become the norm in recent years because it is easy, efficient, and most of the time, free. However, reaching out to your customers through face-to-face interaction creates a multi-dimensional experience that an online experience can't fully replicate. You can use facial expressions, body language and overall vibe in communicating with customers. Take advantage of the personal approach through meetings, networking and events to successfully introduce or bring awareness to your brand.

Is awareness enough? No. You have to persuade customers to make a decision and take action hence the brand engagement process doesn't stop. Remember what people say about relationships? "It takes time. You have to work at it every day."

When your brand engages with people, it has to undergo the whole process from the initial warming up, constant awareness, to interaction until it becomes a habit of shared experiences. In the sales funnel, there are several parts to be followed, and some parts have to be repeated to achieve the results that you want for your brand.

Even customers that were turned off once and didn't go back to your business to avail of your services can be engaged again through an eye-catching advertisement. In business, you must never give up because your customers are human beings with minds and hearts that can be attracted, persuaded and won over. All it takes is perseverance and a certain amount of creativity and imagination to get them hooked on your marketing initiatives.

Do you have to create a website or have social media platforms for your business to succeed today? It is a great step to take and worth, but these options are not the only ones that work. Your brand also needs to build long-lasting connections through offline channels and methods that go the extra mile to let customers experience something unique and remarkable.

Masterfully Connect Online

Nowadays, there's no denying the phenomenal wave of different brands thriving in an online and global platform. The internet is a playground for businesses and brands to test the waters and try new ways to engage with their customers. Brands, big and small, are putting up accounts and pages on Facebook, Instagram and LinkedIn to be noticed and recognized. The people are responding to their interactions and it's exciting. Some experts comment on the saturation of brands online and the intense competition, but I believe digital is the future.

Should you plunge in because others have? The story goes back to your brand and what it stands for. What have you got to gain from the shift from offline to online? If you're selling a physical product, there are many ways to market it online. You can also pique the interest of your customers through social media interaction.

When it comes to successful brand engagement, the online presence can significantly help. Through your own personal or business website, you can tell your story which makes it easier for people to relate to you even on a personal level. Your website is a powerful tool to attract attention and keep customers interested in a long time. As with every initiative, it requires consistent effort and communication. Your online content should be relevant to what's happening all around or should have a timeless appeal, so people are engaged.

HOW IMPORTANT IS BRAND ENGAGEMENT?

You may have heard of brand engagement mentioned several times in marketing meetings, but the entire concept's significance to your business may not be that apparent. Do you want to know the importance of brand engagement and the multitude of benefits that it can contribute to your success?

In this book, I want to open your mind to the possibility of maximizing the potential of engaging and connecting with your customers. But I will share first what you can expect if your business has limited to zero brand engagement.

EFFECTS OF POOR BRAND ENGAGEMENT

Impersonal Customer Interaction

We present our personal or corporate brand in order to communicate with our audience, the people we want to reach. However, in our business, if we don't know how to engage with our customers, we tend to have miscommunication and poor customer service. These are not good signs if you want to have a thriving business that is patronized by your community and your entire target market.

Humanizing your interaction with your customers is very important to establish a long-lasting connection. As mentioned before, your customers are human beings, and they can see and feel if you're not engaging with them, or just going through the motions. Even if you have trained your staff with the best customer service skills and if they are just memorizing lines when talking to customers, your store or business will not be a place of memorable experiences. You will not leave a great impression, and your customers will just come and go. They will not be compelled to return to your store especially if other stores have mastered the art of brand engagement better than yours.

Misinterpretation of Market Needs

Brand awareness is a valuable concept for a business to pursue but it's only the initial step. What if people know about your brand but they feel intimidated because of the information available? What if your restaurant aims to cater to medium-income people but they are misinformed? The next step is brand engagement because if you don't fix the issue, you will be wondering for a long time why your target customers are not frequenting your restaurant.

A great way to engage with people is to join food bazaars and events to market your menu and get immediate feedback from personal interactions with customers. This applies to other types of businesses as well. Remember that if you just stick to brand awareness, you might misinterpret what your customers want and need. Posts on social media platforms can help as well because you get feedback when you need it regarding the performance of your public speaking event, other events or maybe of your daily operations for example. Through the exchange of ideas between brand and customers, many challenges and issues can be solved or even prevented from happening.

Limited Brand Recall

Now it's easy to establish brand recall through offline and online methods but imagine if you have brand engagement strategies in place that don't actually work. You will be wasting time, effort and money, and customers will not even remember your brand. Plan your next move otherwise you will be swallowed whole by your competition. If your brand doesn't register in the hearts and minds of people, they will just forget you and go for the brand that cares for them.

Brand recall is essential in securing your credibility because if you have put that in place, it means customers have an automatic positive response to what you have to offer. For example, A lot of people go to a specific marketing agency because they have a powerful, relevant and engaging brand. Every time you need something done for your business, you reach out to them because you remember that they were reliable, efficient and excellent in terms of customer service. You cannot underestimate that kind of loyalty. Even if that agency commits a bad work, you don't believe the news right away because your experience with them was pleasant. With a lack of proper engagement, you lose customers quickly and that means a negative thing for your business.

Low Number of Recurring Customers

With a failing brand engagement strategy, you will have one or two-time customers who don't really care about your business. They just care about their own needs being fulfilled. Remember that engagement is communication between brand and customers. If the customers don't value your worth, they also treat your products and services in a self-serving way. If they get what they want, they leave.

As a dentist for example, if you don't engage or establish rapport with your patients, they can go for treatment once or twice but will not return and will never ask their families and friends to see you as well. The referral chain breaks. It is the same with other professions and even freelance artists who want to establish a personal/professional brand to gain more customers/audience and have sustainable careers. It's true that "word of mouth" is still relevant and useful. On social media, it is the system that works. People online tell other people what they like and recommend through statuses, pictures and videos. This is how vital brand engagement is; when you fail at it, your customers – lifeblood of your business – will not be accessible to you. They will not return to you when your services or products are needed. They will look somewhere else, and we have to prevent that from happening through the right methods of engagement and connection.

Mediocre Sales and Profits

Expect a domino effect when you don't incorporate the right engagement strategies. It will get worse, and your sales will suffer. A genuine connection with customers can be the determining factor for the success of your business in terms of sales and profits. Your brand or business was created to launch your services, products or even your great ideas. You have an end goal and that includes financial income and return on investments. Before you can reach that goal, you need to hustle. You have to employ business strategies that increase brand awareness and attract more customers.

The next step is to build a bridge between your ideas and your customers' feedback. This is where engaging with customers is important. Without this crucial element, you're not adhering to an effective flow of launching, advertising, marketing, selling and of course, profiting from your business. Everything you do in your business should ultimately result in higher sales and profit otherwise you cannot help your customers anymore or improve their lives because you are out of business. The relationship should be the mutualism kind and you have to know your role in the equation by heart so as to avoid a failing business.

Business Longevity Is At Risk

The last effect of poor brand engagement that we are trying hard to combat is the failure of your brand or corporate business. It doesn't matter if it's online or offline, a business entity will suffer the consequences of complacency and lack of regard for customer engagement soon if the challenge is not faced head-on. You will no longer have a business to grow, scale or develop if you don't pay close attention to the effective ways of brand engagement.

The issue is personal because you might lose hope and be disappointed in yourself for this failure of reaching your goal. Also, it involves a lot of people because if your business operation stops, your employees will be out of jobs. Some businesses are content with the status quo and mediocre sales but if there are innovative ways to secure success and longevity, wouldn't you be eager to try them?

I think it's high time that we expand our imagination and explore the possibilities of brand engagement. What benefits will it bring to your business? With your brand, how can you apply best practices to see great results sooner? Let's check out the next chapter and see where your open and eager mind will lead you.

4

BENEFITS OF CONNECTING WITH CUSTOMERS

We advocate exceptional brand engagement because people can decide to buy, avail of, or support services and products that inspire a human connection especially an emotional one. For our bonds with our customers to be long-lasting, a great foundation should be in place first. Through consistent nurturing, they don't even have to be persuaded. They come to you with open arms.

A long-established brand, many battles to achieve it and some attain it, however, behind it all are hours and hours of planning. A great brand does not come up overnight but is resultant of extensive thoughtfulness in the whole process. Be it the toddler footsteps of a brand or the overall growth, the backbone of the brand is its brand engagement.

One of the key benefits of brand engagement is hastening the decision-making process of customers. They don't have to think much of what they are going to do next. If they know your brand well and are familiar with your brand story, and relates to your experiences, possibilities are high that they will buy your products even if they are new or expensive. They trust your brand. They are confident that what you offer will benefit their lives.

SUCCESSFUL BRAND ENGAGEMENT BENEFITS

Mastering the art of brand engagement certainly provides a multi-faceted list of benefits. It targets all areas of customer relationship beyond brand awareness and marketing. Ultimately, it involves more responsive customer service because of access to the customers' thoughts and comments.

Brand engagement is a holistic approach and yields results that encompass a sustainable brand-customer connection. I am sharing with you these benefits so you can better understand the difference that brand engagement can provide for your business.

Heightened Brand Awareness

After launching your brand and sharing your story with the world, you have to proactively engage with people especially the one belonging to your target market. Every time you are in the presence of customers, you have to keep in mind your brand's identity and character and embody them in your interaction. Your staff in your shop, office, social media or any commercial establishment should represent your brand with consistency to increase the awareness.

Your brand is an evolving entity. Your brand character is not static hence you can't remain the same if customers are rejecting the idea of what you stand for. This is where feedback comes in. Listen to what your customers say and respond appropriately to establish confidence and trust. The deeper your connection to them, the more heightened your brand awareness will be. Your customers can no longer dismiss you as just one of the brands; you become their go-to brand for their needs. And that is an excellent place to be, in the high esteem of your customers.

Remarkable Brand Reputation

Brand engagement when done properly and successfully can enhance reputation to a significant degree. This is vital in establishing trust with customers. In attracting prospective clients, this is important, because even if they haven't encountered your brand yet if they have heard good things about it from friends, family and people in their circle, they are bound to feel secure and confident. A connection has already been built that if nurtured further can lead to a promising future for your brand.

The impact of engagement to your brand reputation is so immense that it can alleviate some of the areas that you're not excelling at such as product advertising or marketing. If done right, sometimes, you don't need to exert too much effort in these areas because customers can already count on your products and your capacity to deliver. With that, you should still be able to balance every factor and not just focus on engagement completely. A solid reputation is very important but I hope you don't neglect the quality of your offerings as well. You can address this area and improve your products and services through brand engagement strategies that get the recommendations straight from your customers' mouths.

Access to Valuable Feedback

Studies have shown that an estimated 60% of customers will go to other brands if they encounter an improved customer service from those brands. This is eye-opening and a perfect reason not to be complacent. With a brand engagement effort that works, your access to feedback from customers is easy or comments may even be unsolicited most of the time. Either way, you are the winner because you have an opportunity to assess these feedbacks and improve your services or products based on them.

As a brand entity, make sure that if you ask for feedback, you are open to applying the recommendation later on or sooner. Otherwise, there's no point bothering to ask them in the first place. Your customers will be happy to give comments if they think they will be useful for your brand. Just to reiterate, brand engagement is a connection between your brand and your customers so every encounter with them should be amiable, positive and beneficial.

If your business is new, this is particularly helpful because you might be knowledgeable about the industry but you may not be updated with what customers are truly looking for these days. The millennial crowd has a different set of preference compared to the generation that came before. Consider it a sign of great rapport when customers post their feedback online or tell it directly to you or your staff. It means they feel comfortable and your response should be positive too.

Secure Customers' Loyalty

One of the most important benefits of brand engagement is customer loyalty. This factor cannot be bought and you cannot trick customers into being loyal to your brand.

Is the development of loyalty organic? You can make it happen through the sincere effort of reaching out to your customers and strengthening their trust. According to Accenture, 51% of customers are responsive to brands that engage with them through various communication channels and they become loyal to these brands. The good news is that you can improve your interaction with customers and show authentic care for their welfare in order for them to bestow their loyalty to your brand.

Loyalty in a brand and customer relationships are extremely important for the growth of your brand. It gives you hope to move forward and pursue the direction that you have planned for your business or company. Even if customers are being courted and impressed by other brands, if your bond with them is strong, they will not be easily persuaded. They will be reluctant to change course but you have to revitalize your ties through other forms of engagement otherwise they will reconsider. In business, as in life, there is no guarantee of forever, but through consistency and perseverance, you can count on good results. Before you know it, decades have passed but your business is still flourishing. Maintain a positive attitude about your growth.

Customer Retention

This benefit is similar to customer loyalty but this is much more actionable. You can recapture your customers' attention through brand engagement and retain their interest and loyalty. A study by Aberdeen Group Inc. concluded that companies that engage their customers effectively through different channels get 89% customer retention. This means that by taking the initiative to appreciate your customers through rewards offline or prizes and activities online, they can feel that you're taking the time to recognize their worth. You are with them as they experience your brand in different avenues and settings. Brand loyalty rewards are also effective ways to retain your customers for a longer period of time.

Recurring customers are definitely assets for brands and businesses especially in the beginning when you still have something to prove. It encourages you to continue what you're doing right. For entrepreneurs and companies that have been around for years, they also need these customers to be more sustainable because the world is changing rapidly. The products and services that people need evolve and by having recurring customers, you secure the future of your business, and at the same time, you can keep everything fresh and updated through their experiences and ideas.

Consistent Positive Response to New Offerings

It's true that even the biggest brands in the world can make a mistake and launch a product that will flop. But with today's advanced technology in market research and manufacturing, this rarely happens anymore. Nike is consistent in launching successful products time and time again. The brand has the most sophisticated brand engagement system in place. It works and people can see that. For a new business or brand, this can be intimidating. After launching a product that performed well, you might be thinking about the reaction of your customers to your next products. That is to be expected but you can limit the pressure when you build anticipation for new products through engagement online or press releases spread in print.

Unveiling a new product is no longer daunting when you have already set the expectations of your customers or target market. They know something exciting and new is coming and before launching the product, you have already done your market research through their active interaction and contribution. When customers are nurtured, entertained and engaged consistently, you can count on the positive response to your new offerings. They are familiar with your brand. They know your story by heart. They gravitate to you. Whatever you put in front of them, they will like it. Why? The reason is that you know them by heart, too. You have a clear understanding of what will make them excited and eager. When brand engagement is in complete harmony, you are bound to succeed.

Higher Sales and Business Success

Your ultimate achievement as a business or brand is the success and this can be measured in various ways, the most obvious and most coveted is having higher sales. One of the most effective methods to achieve this, especially in this day and age of immediacy and technological advancement, is through brand engagement. People are restless these days and consumers are always looking for something new. They are expecting faster and better services and more efficient and more innovative products. How can you increase your sales when you are pressured and you feel as if you're at the mercy of consumers? You befriend your consumers and engage them with the original offering of your brand.

When you go the extra mile to differentiate your brand from the rest by delving deeper into the psyche of your customers, you have a higher chance of succeeding. The focus doesn't have to be purely for your customers alone. Unfortunately, by focusing entirely on target markets, we forget that brand awareness is equally essential. Create high-quality products that meet your standards and fulfill the needs of your customers, and you will notice that you also started serving people outside your expected target markets. It's a win-win situation! Through this strategy, you can boost your sales and through recurring customers, you can maintain or increase you profits.

GAURAV GULATI

5

STRATEGIES THAT CONQUER CONSUMER'S HEARTS

Building and developing a brand is not just about impersonal business strategies. Most of the time, what we fail to do is to appeal to the emotions of our customers. Discovering the concept of brand engagement is such a game-changer in the world of business and branding. Nowadays, everyone wants to know how to conquer their customers' hearts efficiently. We realize now that emotional connection is what triggers customer response to a particular brand. The challenge is to tug at the heartstrings of our customers in a sincere way.

Numerous brands are employing manipulative strategies, but to stand out from the phonies, you have to recognize the value of your customers in your business. You have to realize that they truly matter. Your existence is essential to them and the same is true about their worth to your brand.

BRING VALUE TO CUSTOMER'S LIVES

"People don't care how much you know until they know how much you care." - Theodore Roosevelt

Informing the world of your existence is not your final goal as a brand. You have to define your brand through the value that you can provide to customers. How can you transform their lives for the better? This is the ultimate type of brand engagement. You are not just involved in your brand-customer interaction. You are committed to adding value to their lives. Let's see how you can make that happen through these effective steps:

IDENTIFY THEIR PROBLEMS

How can you help your customers if they don't realize they need your assistance? If you know the people who can benefit from your brand then you are also aware of their problems. Identify them through your specialized knowledge. For example, you can point out that they have beautiful skin and their sunspots can be eliminated through laser removal. As a result, they can have smoother and more radiant skin. It's a subtle approach but you have already caught their attention, and they are interested to know if you offer this service in your skin treatment clinic.

PROVIDE SOLUTIONS

If you're a customer, what will you choose, the easier route or the difficult one? You will definitely choose the former. If you have already identified whatever problems a customer has, you can recommend a solution. You are in the best position to help them solve problems. They don't have to look for solutions themselves because you're already there to guide them. You are ready to help and they are willing to be helped. You didn't push a product in their faces without establishing a need for it first. This method makes them feel that you're doing them a favour and they are appreciative of it.

SHOW THEM RESULTS

Customers who buy your products or avail your services are investing money for results that they wish to see. If they buy a blender from you, will it make their food preparation faster and breakfast more delicious? How about if they purchase a bottle cutter, will they be able to make creative home decors that they can sell on Amazon or on their own store? What are the results when they invest in what your brand has to offer? Show them so that they can make informed decisions and they will realize that you have provided suggestions and even unsolicited advice that will benefit them.

GIVE THEM ALTERNARIVES

If you notice that your customers have been wearing jackets that belong in the same trend category, you can help them see other options. Ask them if they want to experiment with their wardrobe and show them alternatives. Make their shopping experience more fun and engaging. Help them to feel good about their bodies and their fashion choices. Whatever your business, you are bound to find alternative products, services or methods that your customers might find more helpful compared to the previous ones that they have tried. Don't leave all the decisions to them. Step up the plate and be proactive in letting them know that your brand can take care of their needs.

COLLABORATE WITH THEM

Even the most unsociable customers can melt with your helpful ways. There's a balanced approach that you can use without overstepping your boundaries. Train your staff to be friendly but not intrusive. No one wants a saleslady that follows you every turn you take at a boutique. Let them keep a comfortable distance but always within earshot so that they can assist when the customers need help right at that moment. Your staff has to be knowledgeable about what they're selling so they can collaborate with your customers in terms of accessories choices, for example.

INVEST IN CUSTOMER EXPERIENCE

Have you been so focused on your products and services that you haven't paid attention to the experience of your customers? According to a White House Office of Consumer Affairs research, 80% of consumers in America are willing to spend more just to have a customer experience that's superior from the rest. We can't neglect this crucial part of the brand engagement. Let's take the initiative and go out of our way to make sure that our brand provides a memorable experience for our customers.

Create Interactive Surveys

Some customer surveys just put people to sleep. They don't want to answer them because they don't spark any interest. Make your surveys interactive and exciting. Or make them personal and heartwarming. Ask questions about their family and loved ones. These are beneficial surveys and ad campaigns that involve stories of rags to riches, undying hope, unrequited love, etc. Don't underestimate your customers' capacity to empathize with your message as a brand.

Customer Challenges

Do you have doubts about how much your customers love your products? You are not alone because many entrepreneurs stay up all night wondering the same thing that's why you have to be proactive. Persuade customers to join fun challenges that involve your brand. How about fun runs or triathlon events? If your business is in the health and wellness industry, then this is a fantastic idea to get customers energized and engaged.

Nonprofit Initiative

If your brand is supporting a charity, this is a wonderful way to engage your customers and encourage them to participate. You can invite them in fundraising initiatives so that they can feel involved and valued enough for you to share such a fulfilling experience with them. Your brand cannot be a stagnant entity. It should also participate in the community through these worthwhile efforts and in this way, you can meet and engage with your consumers.

RELATE WITH VIP CUSTOMERS

One valuable strategy that I can share with you is to nurture your special relationship with your VIP customers. They are people who have been supporting you for years and their loyalty is paramount. They provide consistent sales and most of the time, give you worthy feedback. Make sure you are gracious in receiving those and respond according to their wishes. You can incorporate some of these ways to take care of your VIP customers.

Behind-the-Scenes Access: If you're an entrepreneur promoting your business and you are organizing a music concert or fashion show for example, you can reward VIP customers with backstage passes. They will appreciate the gesture and enjoy the experience, and naturally, will associate the memories with your brand.

Special Treatment: In a beauty salon or spa clinic, you can give massive discounts to your VIP clients or give them free services after they have availed of a series of services within a period of time. Everyone feels excited when they get freebies, and high-paying clients feel the same. They don't just relish the experience; they also tell their friends about it and that's free marketing for your brand.

Engage in Feedback and Surveys: The best people to ask for feedback from are your most loyal customers. The familiarity with your brand is already there and they have experienced your services firsthand numerous times. They are also in a position to know about the changes that your brand has undergone through the years. All you have to do is send them an e-mail, call them or talk to them in person. Give them an incentive for answering your surveys such as free tickets or deliver a basket of goodies or discounts. Personalizing your communication with your VIP customers will tug at their hearts and endear your brand to them even more.

Customize Message to Customers: Absolutely no one wants to receive a generic sales message from a brand. People might read it but resonating with it is another story. Hence, you have to take the initiative to customize your message when you reach out to your customers. You can use the first name of your recipients for an e-mail newsletter. Make the tone conversational and helpful otherwise they will not hesitate to click the unsubscribe button. Similarly, in personal interactions in your store or office, you can use a polite designation and initiate conversation but make sure your small talk is helpful and friendly. In your customized updates or press releases to customers, you can provide links to other websites that can further help them in their daily life or include informative tips and advice. You can even engage them by asking them to join fun runs, music festivals, shopping bazaars, etc. One of the research studies figured out that customers who are consistently engaged "are five times more likely to buy only from the same brand in the future". Take advantage of this knowledge by nurturing your relationship with your customers through messages and interactions that are not manipulative, but helpful and persuasive instead.

You can't go wrong when you reach out to the human side of your customers. When you approach them not merely as your customers but people who are capable of loyalty, support and compassion, they recognize that your brand is good to them. It's great to feel that you and the people who love your brand are on the same page.

GAURAV GULATI

6

WINNING BRAND ENGAGEMENT

Brand engagement now is very different than that of the past, and today people have a lot of expectations because of numerous choices. Brand engagement creates a deeply emotional and rational connection between business, employees, and customers. It helps in building a stronger brand and thus promote business.

The concept of brand engagement encourages us to take risks that offer promising rewards. If you stay where you are and not exert effort in communicating with your customers, you will not see the great possibilities of developing your brand on a local or even global scale. I have these amazing tips that are often ignored by most brands because they are too obvious or too tedious to do.

Are you ready to take risks?

Some methods require you to think out of the box and use your imagination. The world of business has become more competitive and being bold and courageous to try new ways of engagement is what's going to drive you forward. Be open to trying these tips and watch your brand become more relevant and memorable to your customers.

GRATITUDE STILL WORKS

When brands offer their services and products to people, they are thanked because they gave something of value or helped improve lives. But do brands return the favour and show gratitude to their customers for keeping them alive and thriving? Most brands do but not in a way that people can really see the gesture. Be creative with how you thank your customers. Call them a few days before Christmas not to sell them anything but just to say "Thank you." They would appreciate the gesture because it has no strings attached. You can give them treats in your store before they leave, not to advertise a new product but just to make them smile. It works!

ENGAGE IN CREATIVE ART

A provocative print ad can spark conversations about your brand. People would talk about your advertisement if you gave them something to think about or feel. Don't limit your marketing efforts to the usual methods. Think out of the box and your customers will surely want to share their opinions about your ads with their friends, family or even strangers on the street. It's a great way to spread the word. On social media, people can just take photos of your print ad and share them on their Facebook or Instagram etc. Your brand gets exposure and engagement because consumers think that you're inviting them to a conversation, a meaningful interaction.

GET CUSTOMERS INVOLVED

Your customers love your brand. They want to know what's fresh and cool about you. If you're running out of creative ideas, then you have these great people to help you. Let them pick out colours for new cellphone cases that you're creating. Make them choose designs that they're excited about. Ask them about photography themes that they want to see come to life. When you value the ideas of your customers, it shows that you are willing to give them exactly what they want. Your products will be better than you've imagined because your customers' ideas are incorporated in them. Brands should not be boring. Find out ways to keep your audience entertained and engaged through collaboration and having fun together.

SHARE, INFORM, HELP

You've chosen to launch, grow and develop a brand in a specific industry. Naturally, you have more knowledge than your customers about this area and you can engage with them by sharing free information and advice. It could be in the form of a small pamphlet, comics, book of inspiration, etc. If you give them these gifts at an unexpected circumstance, they will realize that you know this industry by heart and you care enough to share, educate or inform them about it. In a drugstore, this kind of gesture will be greatly appreciated because health tips, medical success stories will give people hope. It invites people to ask for help and your staff is there to make them feel that they have come to the right place.

MENTORSHIP INITIATIVES

Do you think the idea of mentorship is time-consuming? Do you think it's a waste of energy to invest such time and effort just to keep customers engaged? The good news is it's worth your effort and it's not as tedious as you might think. If your personal brand caters to amateur photographers or copywriters, you can present your clients with mentors who are part of your staff or you can be their mentors in a one-time or monthly event. These clients have tons of questions for you and as you answer them, you will also know how to improve your service offering through the ideas that they ask about.

PERSONALIZE YOUR IMAGE

When people hear the word "transaction", they are reluctant to go out of the house. When they hear "dental appointment", they think of ways to postpone it. Why? People think it's a chore and they don't feel connected to authority figures or intimidating brands. The trick is to get your receptionist or staff to present you to patients in a more personal way. She can describe you as a warm, caring dentist who often has funny jokes. As a professional, you can also build rapport by sharing anecdotes about your personal life. Don't hesitate to share appropriate stories about family and life because your clients or patients have families too.

PUT YOUR HEART OUT

The same principle applies in this area: show your heart. Be personal. Be open. If you're a creative artist who sells paintings, collages and murals, your art can speak for you but sometimes your patrons want to have access to the behind the scenes. They want to know what inspired you to create such art. You can't just put a one-line caption to your creation. Make it a personal message to art enthusiasts. Raise a question in your message that asks them their emotional and creative outlet. That's the beginning of a beautiful conversation with them.

SOCIAL MEDIA FIRE

Reaching out to customers through social media is sure to cause a fire of ideas, insights and engagement. Through Twitter, Facebook, YouTube and Instagram, you can already launch your brand and it's convenient to spread your influence through pictures and video posts. This engagement method is also free at the onset, unless you want to launch a massive social media campaign. You can start with simply updating your status and asking your circle to recommend or suggest ideas for your brand. It's human nature to help someone in need and it's a natural reaction for people to respond if the topic you put out there piques their interest. Take the initiative from there and monitor the progress of your brand in terms of advertising, engaging and connecting with relevant people on your social media platforms. Don't forget to enjoy because people gravitate to others who have a positive attitude!

COMPELLING VIDEO STORIES

Emotional ads from creative marketers hailing from different parts of the world like Thailand, India, England, China, just to name a few, are rapidly circulating online. As human beings, our hearts need to be touched in order to be engaged with brands that feel like part of our lives already. Your brand can follow suit and work with creative directors and visual storytellers who can create heartwarming videos of the real face of life – with suffering, struggles, love and compassion. It doesn't have to be an expensive endeavor. Remember, your customers can take part in this creative project. They can help you here and you can help them in return. It's a vulnerable yet open bond between brand and customers.

When your brand engagement efforts end for the day, you can enjoy the peace of knowing that your customers are sharing good things about you to their friends and family. You have entered their lives through sincere and consistent connection and they know who you are and what you stand for as an engaging, entertaining and empowering brand.

7

STRATEGIES THAT BOOST BRAND ENGAGEMENT

Have you ever found yourself stuck in an uninteresting conversation with someone who seems to talk only about themselves? Their interests, achievements, issues, solutions and after a while, you begin to tune them out You might have noticed that a good conversation is more like tennis, where both players hit the ball, with appropriate questions and helpful, thoughtful, authentic answers moving back and forward in a timely fashion. When both sides are engaged in this way, everyone has a good time.

Brands in the social media space who seek to form an ongoing connection with their audience should observe the same rules of graciousness when planning and executing a social media strategy. The purpose of social media is not just to tell your audience how great you are, but to emphasize how important they and their feedback are to your brand.

When you are crafting your brand engagement plan for social media don't keep just one goal in mind, it should be able to do different things for you at different time and day. Increase Sales, Create Stronger Brand Identity, Create Brand Awareness, Get More Sign-Ups for your Newsletter, Get Feedbacks etc. Having specific goal can ultimately damage the engagement process, as the same audience has different needs and areas of interest, so keeping the balance in everything is very important.

The engaging audience can provide multiple benefits:

- You can get people talking about your brand
- You can learn more about your existing customers
- You can learn more about potential customers
- You can learn more about your competitors

Based on the above benefits you can develop new marketing strategies to communicate with both your existing and potential customers more efficiently in the future. To acquire these benefits, you must be prepared to engage your audience with various entertaining methods that benefit your customers.

TACTICS YOU CAN TRY TODAY TO INCREASE YOUR BRAND ENGAGEMENT ONLINE:

Ask Questions

Engage your audience with appropriate questions, in the form of Twitter, Instagram and Facebook posts, and polls. Don't worry about asking questions that particularly relate to your brand, but rather, questions that people on your space would be interested in answering so that the result is increased engagement. You can use keyword trackers like Wordtracker to decide the questions your patrons are already asking around a specific subject. Questions can be posted to the audience via Twitter, Instagram, Facebook, LinkedIn or in the form of surveys, polls and quizzes. The more you ask, the more engagement you'll get, and if your brand can sustain posing daily questions, you will have people coming back to check for new questions and answers on the regular. You will witness fantastic response if these questions are attached to discounts, coupons or free goodies. This will build up your regular audience and a high level of brand engagement.

Host a Live Chat

Invite the audience to join a real conversation around a topic related to your brand. If you have new product, service or have issues or concerns, you can contact your audience live and talk with them in real time with a personal touch. Make sure you keep content relevant, keep it going, keep it exciting, and keep it clean. The best part is that you don't require special software to experiment with the elements of live chat, this can be included into your existing social media. But, yes to make it more victorious you probably can start promoting your Live Session in advance to make it much more successful and engaging. For example; brands like Oneplus, Buzzfeed, Dunkin Donuts are using Live Streaming the most to engage their audience. We all understand that video is one of the most engaging content formats, and live streaming makes it even better as it also opens the door to live feedback.

Offer A Deal or Promotion

Create engagement by offering deals and promotions. Fact is over 54% of social media users follow at least one brand. According to several studies surprisingly the main reason why most people follow brands is to "Get a Special Offer". So, a highly efficient way to boost engagement is to play to that desire. Offer small and big deals regularly to make your readership base and get them coming back to your digital space. It's not essential to give away only your brand products or services—any product or service (movie tickets, ice cream, cab rides etc.) that is attractive to your preferred audience will achieve your goal of driving engagement. Partner with other brands to offer deals together for some added value and cross promotion. Consider inviting your customers and target audience to follow, friend, or become a fan of your social networking space or e-newsletter to become eligible for deals and promotions.

Create Game

Increase the engagement of a particular target audience, and emphasize a specific message of the brand, with a custom-made online game. Before you select this option, review the cost as game development can be expensive. Look for opportunities to cross-promote with a game company if possible. Make sure the game developed for your brand communicates your brand message and conveys what you want to say. Gamification is a great marketing way to get the audience excited about engaging with you. People enjoy making points, and many brands have combined loyalty programs to these games. Starbucks also has its own game version of the gamified loyalty program.

Run Contest

A robust social media contest can create real value for your brand. One of the most common ways to run a social media contest is to just give away a prize to one your followers randomly, but you can make it more interesting by just doing those giveaways at random and surprising your followers with those prizes. This will help you gaining more fans and followers, improving brand visibility, identity, and driving more traffic to your website. Then look for ways to use cross-promotion to up the visibility and participation in your contest.

Posts Photos And Videos

According to various studies it is proven that over 65% of people are mainly visual learners, they say that a picture is worth a thousand words, and it's true. You can use images and videos to say something about your brand, invite opinions, tagging, and sharing. Studies also show that photos and videos generate up to 200% higher engagement rate than links do on social media. You can post behind-the-scenes pictures and videos, newly decorated space, new projects, new designs, brand history, brand milestones, new menus, new services, facts, inspirational and motivational content etc. but and make sure you keep the content fun and real, add voiceover whenever possible.

Host Guest Post

Find experts or collaborators willing to cross-promote your interests with exciting new content, and add credibility to your brand with a guest posting. This works two ways; you can post content on a partner's social media, or you can enlist a relevant personality to post on your space. Brands might partner with influencers, or more established brands to gain credibility, or older brands might want to partner with individuals or companies to prove their brand's relevance. It's also an excellent way for bloggers to gain more exposure. Opportunities are everywhere!

#Hashtag

According to Philip Kotler #Hashtag is the new tagline. Hashtags are everywhere these days, these expand your reach outside your network, engage with your followers, open new ways of communicating and boost brand awareness and engagement. In today's business strategy hashtag and brand engagement for your brand conjointly exist to make it successful. When we began with this internet transformation, it was used in social media sites to project point of views and/or opinions. However current times have seen it part of your branding strategy to reach the audience. With the rise of Tweeting, the hashtag started to become the new mode of communication with the world in daily lives. One hashtag in any one of the account be it Twitter, Instagram or Google plus can help you enter the world of the hashtag and reach out your audience despite the fact that they are following you or not. In short, the hashtag is the new tagline for your company to flourish. Just like every business has a catchy tagline for textual advertisement; similarly, the tech-savvy form of advertisement for your business is none other than hashtags.

Now, what are these much-talked hashtags? Hashtags are word or phrases written with a symbol of # to be used on social media websites and applications for message categorization under specific topic A impactful tagline written with a hashtag symbol is the next generation branding strategy to boost brand engagement through social media websites and applications.

With the simple formation of two or three words, your hashtag can help your business to keep track of your brand on social media. The best way to get the masses attention is through hash symbol followed by structured words. It also helps as a medium of communication between potential and existing consumers and your brand to boost brand engagement. Branding your business through hashtags would help you in creating a long-lasting perception regarding your brand. It also assists business in trending industry news in real time to be updated. Of course, the hashtag is another sales generation strategy for your business.

Begin by creating your brand specific hashtag which would reflect your business, make it around your company name while keeping it unique. Make your hashtag answer the question of what is trending now to make it viral among the audience. You can also incorporate hashtags for the content of your posts to make it SEO friendly and better advertising. In order to communicate with your users, one can use chat hashtags. When a specific action involving your brand is required, call to action hashtag comes into the picture. The whole step of creating your hashtag strategy begins with figuring out the identity of your business, create some drafts, then research your hashtag from the purpose to be solved and finally make a choice.

SOCIAL MEDIA DON'Ts

- **Don't** provide confidential, proprietary or customer information.
- **Don't** post more than one time in a day and more than 7 posts in a week, over posts can saturate your audience. This rule shall not be applicable during product/service launch, contest or on special events.
- **Don't** forget that brand is represented by its people and what you publish represent your brand.
- **Don't** violate copyright, fair use, privacy or financial disclosure laws.
- **Don't** express your opinions on political parties, politicians, celebrities and religions.

GAURAV GULATI

8

NEGATIVE BRAND ENGAGEMENT

This may sound surprising, but it's true there are two types of brand engagement positive and negative engagement. Unfortunately, most of the businesses especially in developing nations are practising negative brand engagement which they never realize. Positively Engaged customers spend much more time and money with brands, and according to various studies, it is seen that engaged customer add around 23% percent profitability, revenue and relationship growth. On the other hand, disengaged customers represent approximately 13% reduction in those same metrics.

HERE ARE SOME EXAMPLES OF HOW ENGAGED CUSTOMERS BEHAVE IN SERVAL INDUSTRIES:

Hotels - Engaged guests spend an average of 46% more per year

Restaurants: Engaged guests visit their favourite restaurant and fast food 56% more often

Insurance: Engaged policyholders buy around 22% more services

Banking: Engaged customers have higher deposit balance and provide approximately 37% more revenue to the bank

Consumer Electronics: Engaged customers visit their favourite store around 44% more often and spend on something or other on their most of the visits.

Don't get me wrong I was only talking about engaged and disengaged customers not about negatively engaged customers. You will be amazed to know that negatively engaged customers can do the lot more damage to the brand than disengaged customers.

LET US UNDERSTAND THE DIFFERENCE BETWEEN POSITIVE AND NEGATIVE BRAND ENGAGEMENT:

POSITIVE BRAND ENGAGEMENT

- A person feels comfortable with the particular brand
- Happily, spend more time with the brand
- Spend more money
- Return back to the brand
- Share positive feedback with their family and friends

NEGATIVE BRAND ENGAGEMENT:

- A person feels uncomfortable with the particular brand
- Scared spending time with the brand
- They usually never shop because of the negative engagement
- Never return back to the brand
- Share negative feedback with their family and friends

I have an excellent example for you; I was looking to buy the property in Chandigarh, India and during this process of searching property I met many real estate agents and builders. I would not hesitate to write it that it was my life's biggest mistake that I shared my mobile number with few of these agents and builders. Most of them phoned me at least 2-3 times a day, and I tried my best explaining most of these people that I need time taking my decision as you don't buy a property every day, it is a lifelong decision, and I want to make it sure that I take the correct decision. Despite this shamelessly most of these people kept calling me again and again, there was a time when I stopped taking their calls and use to cancel the calls, but still, most of these agents called me again and again. Finally, I blocked their numbers on my phone. You will be shocked to know that 2-3 agents called me from different numbers, how foolish and insane one could be? This is Negative Brand Engagement!

I am sorry to write this, but unfortunately, it's not the case only in real estate sector the same is also happening in other industries too. I am sure you must have experienced something similar, it's not my only experience of negative brand engagement. I can never forget the times when I was irritated by one of the world's best self-publishing company and used to get calls from the United States, they too behaved the way real estate agent acted in India.

If calling your customers and potential customers are part of your sales and marketing plan, think again. Research shows calling customers is outdated, disturbing, pushy and most importantly waste of time and energy.

The Australian Institute found Australian spend an average of 147 minutes on telemarketing calls each year. I am sure the number would be much more in most of the developing countries.

Negative brand engagement doesn't happen only through phoning; it also happens when you flood your customers and target audience mailbox with too many emails or when your salesperson stands and walks shoulder to shoulder with the customer in the showroom. People these days are surrounded by hundreds of concerns and stresses, life is running fast; therefore, it is important to give enough space to your customers. I assure you if the brand like Apple would have behaved this way they would have never managed to get this level of success. Ask yourself why is e-commerce industry booming? One of the most important reasons behind their success is convenience and enough space customers get to take their decision. It's not just about pricing; it's about the comfort of buying wholly based on your own choice.

IF;

- Your business phone number is marked as Spam by more than 50 people on True Caller
- More than 50 people unsubscribe from your newsletter or mailing list every week
- More than 50% visitors leave your well-stocked store despite salesperson assistance in less than 2 minutes.

If all of the above or at least one of the above is true for your brand, then it is high time to rethink your brand promotion strategy. Wakeup! You are making Negative Brand Engagement.

Some brands fail to grow because of the negative brand engagement, not giving enough space and time to your customer to think is one the main reasons of destructive engagement.

Research has stated that about 70 percent of negative brand engagement occurs due to negative interactions with employees/staff. Other reasons are delivering of products or services below expected level or zero understanding of the needs also play the role of negative brand engagement for your brand.

With changing times, the engagement channels for your brand has evolved from offline to more online medium. The negative response of any form that your consumer showcases be it online or offline is what negative brand engagement is all about. Also, it must be noted that negative brand engagement is not only about the dissented customer, but it is related to potential customers. There are numerous factors and behaviour that can hamper the engagement of your brand adversely. For example: if you end up calling your customers without an objective, if you are unprepared or if you are unable to build relationships, then surely you are dragging your brand towards negative engagement. Social media can be hampering brand engagement as well if left untracked or without originality in the content. Brand extension is another way to bring in new products under the already set up brand name, however, that can sometimes backfire if your new product is unable to perceive the same brand image as your parent product brand.

Identified the problem, now how to solve it?

Communication is the key step as far as brand engagement is concerned, one needs to remember that it is a two-way street and overdoing it can be harmful to your brand. While reaching out to your potential customers, avoid making attempts to sell your product and services over an unwanted sales call. Don't be pushy to make your sale, go through benefits, however; it can backfire if you do not provide enough time for your customer to make a decision. Ensure to keep the front facing staff for your business presentable and knowledgeable. Keep your communication as real as possible, keep it humanistic and positive.

Brand is your selling point and brand engagement is the relationship between brand and consumer based on trust which is a partial indicator of success of your selling point. In short, it is not rocket science to engage already convinced people by pushing them the right message at the right time.

TIPS TO DRIVE POSITIVE BRAND ENGAGEMENT

It is increasingly hard in a world full of opinionated humans to totally avoid any negative reviews or discussions regarding your brand, and so you must accept that it is going to happen at some point in your business life cycle. Negative brand engagement can lead to damaging your firm's reputation which will lower your customer database and in turn reduce the overall profits of the business, and this is something that you really must try to minimise as a brand. This happens mostly online, with social media, customers can post reviews or create status updates relating to your brand, and it can be seen by thousands of potential clients before you even notice, therefore the internet can be both a useful tool but also a dangerous one too for many businesses. However, this can still happen offline through word of mouth discussions. If negative brand engagement and awareness is something that worries you, then you might want to look at the below tips to prevent this from damaging your brand image:

Don't Ignore Brand Mentions

As you develop your brand, it's inevitable that your name will start appearing in search engines and on social networks, and it's imperative that you start searching and checking for this very regularly. Sometimes these mentions can be harmful, and you will need to have them removed and oppose them. Protect your brand image, however, sometimes they can be positive and beneficial for business and promotion, in that case, you will need to positively engage with the person who mentioned you and thanks them, showing your attentive nature and retaining your good brand image. Either way, it's a great habit to get in to, always search for yourself on google and make a note of what you see, then act accordingly. To ease this work, you can use Google Alerts or Mention (www.mention.com)

Know Your Audience

Perhaps the most crucial part of improving brand engagement is to know your audience thoroughly. You need to know who is reading what you post in terms of marketing and advertising, and you also need to know who is viewing your social media pages. It is easy to forget who is looking at what you post and to save yourself from negative publicity. Knowing your audience means researching to learn who your customers are, get to understand the market sector that you want your brand to appeal to and discover correctly what their needs and desires are. All these things show that you care about the customer and can make for better brand awareness.

Be Consistent

It can be hard for customers, clients or colleagues to trust business or brand that regularly fluctuates in behavior and fails to be consistent. Consistency is vital for any brand whether it is personal or corporate. Consistency is so crucial concerning what you post online and what resources you use offline, you must always use the same logos and same images to create a regular and recognized picture in customers minds, so they know that it's your message and your brand. You may feel you have a great brand but consider the fact that you need to differentiate it from your competitors to succeed, so always be consistent with your authenticity and uniqueness. Consistency creates reliability and reliability creates commitment, which all then leads to a reliable client base and more profitability and productivity for the business.

Don't Strain Your Resources

When it comes to creating positive brand awareness and engagement, remember not to spread yourself too thin. Don't look down all the marketing and advertising avenues all at once. Choose a specific researched area and focus on that. Your brand will not become recognized if you are carrying out small-scale work in so many avenues. However, if you focus on growing known on Facebook and Instagram whilst using local advertising and word of mouth, you can put all your resources into those areas and create a right brand image. Once this is done, then you can move on to further aspects such as Twitter and magazines for example. Never set goals that will most certainly lead you to crash and burn. Always remember what resources you have on hand in terms of money and staff, and make sure you are working within the limits and boundaries.

Reduce Self-Promotion

Self-promotion is great to a certain extent; however, it can annoy customers and essentially put them off your brand. They can even eventually get to the point of dreading engaging with your brand. When it concerns social media, if you over promote yourself, people will either un-follow, hide or block you as you will dominate their personal space and they will feel suffocated. Your brand is then recognized as desperate and pushy. Offline, cut down on the leaflets and don't have your staff chase customers down the street, people hate this, and they will automatically feel an aversion to your brand name. An excellent way to boost your brand and be seen is to promote other causes, which is seen as gestures of good-will and creates the image of a kind and caring nature from your business. In turn, people will also start to promote you!

Respect the Customer Opinion

There is nothing worse than seeing an online argument between what is supposed to be a professional business and their customer. In the event of receiving negative feedback, really try to understand where the customer is coming from and offer sincere apologies. Try to get to their level and work out why they feel this way about your brand. This all mounts to constructive criticism and can help you improve services in the future. Respect your customers and they will respect you.

Overall, there are many ways that you can accidentally create negative brand engagement, so use your knowledge and expertise to always avoid doing this by promoting positive techniques and creating a tremendous and lasting image for your business.

GAURAV GULATI

9

WHY PERSONAL BRANDING MATTERS?

In such a competitive world it is essential to find ways to stand out and show what makes your brand unique. The internet has made it increasingly difficult to distinguish uniqueness and originality as it is now much simpler to find everything by a simple click. Therefore, your competitors are quite on the same level ground as they have products, services, website and a social media presence just like you. That is why it is essential to find ways that can distinguish your personal brand as much as possible because otherwise, you are just going to be another business among thousands of others.

Current volatile and competitive market environment has forced brands to worry more about their customers. The critical moment is when the customer meets the employee of the brand. Today when one goes shopping, irrespective of the brand people buy people first over the product. No matter what is the reputation of the product, if a buyer is satisfied by the people representing the brand, BOOM!! Sale Happens! Let say I may deny buying a BMW, due to the failure of the salesperson to make an impression or provide requisite knowledge while on other I may end up buying SKODA over BMW since the salesperson is able to convince me with right reasons (Here I am talking about the personal brand in salespersons perspective). Hence, for brands, personal branding of everyone associated is equally essential as much as a strong brand.

As an individual one needs to enhance his/her personal brand to boost brand engagement of the company or organization they are associated with, which would indirectly give the right push for his/her career too.

Before we dig into what is the relationship that personal branding and brand engagement holds, let us understand each of these components individually. The exercise by which an individual market oneself and its career as brand are what Personal Branding is all about. On another hand, Brand Engagement is the emotional attachment that a consumer has towards a brand.

Personal branding deals with showcasing individual expertise, define a mission, message and goal, this is what differentiates him/her from the regular pool of people, whereas brand engagement is positive attention or even awareness a brand gets. Through brand engagement communication, perception, experience, quality and delivery of brand promise is showcased. Personal branding is the pathway to reach a brand; it leads to draw attention towards the brand which would drive to an overall increase in profitability for any organization or company. Hence, Yes!! Both personal branding and brand engagement are co-related to each other. The enhancement of one can boost the other for any brand.

Still wondering, how can they be related?

Let us understand better with few examples; on one side if it's the Princess Diana personal brand and other is Kim

Kardashian personal brand, people naturally relate more to the former due to the reflection of compassion from her brand. Today people would trust that brand for their holiday planning which has the highest presence in any travel blogs and social media. Here the travel blogger personal brand is indirectly responsible for the sales of any associated travel company.

Personal branding is about the human element. People feel more connected to personal brands as it is not something cold and heartless machine or just big names of companies, but humans with knowledge, ideas, insights, and opinions. This feature of a human will help people in making decisions and solving problems. And therefore, these days people trust what they feel and not what they just see and hear.

Humans are the face of every brand be it an individual brand, business brand or corporate brand. It is equally essential for people of any profession to build their personal brand because this is what boosts the overall brand engagement, after all, people come first then the product/services. Let say for any organization or company, the emphasis on employee branding would lead to engagement of the brand, here we are talking about brand engagement through personal branding of employees. Personal branding can be anything for an individual be it his online presence, sales pitch or through content marketing etc. Hence nowadays companies are looking into building a personal brand for their executives to attract better deals, enhance customer engagement and help in reputation management.

Usually, business leads created through personal relationships are likely to be converted into sale rather than marketing the corporate brand alone. The vision of any company is resonated better with its employees rather than the brand. Hence it is popularly told that your reputation holds the key to your brand's success. Highlighting the people behind the brand helps develop trust on the brand, personal branding can give a human side to your brand.

A personal brand would help in conveying the best version of yourself to assist customers in decisions regarding your brand. Once people get to know the face behind the business through personal branding, brand engagement grows, and sales take off. In short, the strategy for your business should be pivotal to personal branding for better brand engagement results.

The main concept to be successful is that personal branding and brand engagement go hand in hand and you cannot expect your audience to care about your brand unless you give them an effective and noteworthy personal brand to follow. This applies to any business or organization, regardless of its size, as well as for people who want to stand out, including politicians, public speakers, artists, models. The focus on personal branding ultimately leads to brand engagement. These both rely on one another, and one can safely say that they are just like two parallel interlinked processes. Doing well in one will lead to improvements in the other. That is why it is essential to understand the importance of knowing what you are doing in each respect to have a truly successful personal brand and achieve satisfactory brand engagement.

WHY IS PERSONAL BRANDING NECESSARY?

Steady stream of clients

Gone are those days when people use to only rely on marketing for buying any service or products. Nowadays the entire concept is about clients coming to you rather than you chasing them. You should know to represent yourself to sell your product or service. It is because people trust people more and are more compassionate towards human touch over technologies. A well-built personal brand acts like a magnet that attracts your clients.

Allows you to charge extra money

It is pure economics. More the supply, so the demand. A personal brand helps in building your credibility, which allows you to charge more. You as a personal brand have limited time in the day, so if demand increases for your time, expertise, and skills, you obviously get paid more.

Along with this you understand better you look better you can charge, here we are speaking about showcasing your expertise to your target audience. One way of establishing your personal brand more quickly is by sticking to one specialized niche. Specializing makes you to focus on one specific area, which helps in getting better results. And people pay for results.

Build a network: Building a personal brand is most important for building your network. The stronger your personal branding, the more you get access to an exclusive network of people. For example, let us say that two people want to interview Michael Jordan. According to you, who do you think has a better chance of interviewing MJ one-on-one? Someone who has no personal brand at all or someone like Ellen DeGeneres. I know that MJ has already been on her show, but this is just for example, and so let us assume that none of the two knows MJ personally. Still, Ellen will always have the better chance of interviewing him just because of her branding. And as a result of personal branding, she has access to other world-class businesses and individuals too.

Will get you better, bigger deals

With building your personal brand in a right way, more people will be interested in having businesses and contacts with you. They will want to work with you. Along with the existing clients, a strong personal branding will also attract many others who can offer you better and bigger deals.

I hope this chapter was helpful to you. And I hope now you will be having a better understanding of why personal branding and brand engagement go hand in hand.

10

IMPACT AND INFLUENCE OF CULTURE

Today when we walk into an Mc Donald's outlet here in India, you would find either chicken burgers or veg burgers made up of potatoes. While you walk into the same outlet in either US or UK, you would predominantly find beef burgers. Mc Donald's as a brand when began its business it was mainly selling hamburgers, but when this brand extended its roots in other nations like India, China and UAE etc. changes were made for proper brand positioning and engagement in these markets. Ever wondered, why this change? This change is none other than an adaptation of a brand keeping in mind the culture of the market it is selling its products in.

Culture!! How?

To be more elaborative about how culture influences a brand and brand engagement, let's understand it from the above example. As in India, over 50% of the population consider cow as a holy animal, hence cow slaughter is restricted. In order to respect this cultural difference, changes were made in the menu for Mc Donald's in India. Thus it is understood that culture of any area of focus can really impact the brand or its engagement in that said area. To be precise, it is certain that the brand and its engagement is directly proportional to the culture of your targeted consumers. MC Donald's is not the only brand, if you examine you will learn that every intelligent brand makes sure that they understand the culture of their target markets.

Before understanding the relationship between these two, let's first understand each of the terms individually. The brand is that unique identity by which the products or services of your business is recognized. Now the emotional connect that a consumer has towards the brand is what brand engagement is all about. While culture, on the other hand is the characteristics, custom or social behavior of a specific area of people or society gained over a period. The fundamental question that arises now is how we can develop the brand and boost brand engagement by understanding the culture of our consumers?

Now let's dig deep into what impact culture plays on brand and brand engagement

Culture is the behavior pattern or characters of a specific group of people in a particular region. Characteristics can be stretched to religious beliefs, laws, traditions, intellects, or morals. When businesses look out for developing a brand or boosting brand engagement, culture is one of the attributes to look out for. Why? Just like a brand is the sole identity which defines the business similarly culture is the deep-rooted origin of an individual which is displayed in their beliefs, habits, fashion, morals etc.

Hence whenever a brand is being built, it is crucial for organizations to revolve it around the influence of the targeted region to set its foot right. It helps in creating authenticity in your brand in its own way as it is customized towards being specific. The cultural blending not only reduces risks around brand growth but also helps in maximum boosting of brand engagement. The most prominent example which would help one understand the impact of culture on brand and brand engagement is the adaptation of international brands by Indian market due to customization of these brands as per cultural diversification of India. Along with various factors involved in brand building, the impact of the culture of the consumer and region on the brands would support of equal importance.

Cultural marketing should be the part of brand strategies as culturally inclined set of people possess more purchasing power. The connect which develops from cultural vast is predominant to last longer hence also enhance brand engagement and loyalty. Every business should understand if culture comes first, then the performance of your brand will surely follow. Thus it would be undoubtedly concluded that Yes!! Of course, cultural differences would positively or negatively impact a brand.

Giving importance to culture always creates an edge for your brand. However, while cultural diversification is an attribute to be part of branding strategy while entering new markets, the originality of the brand is essential to be maintained as that is the sole reason for their acceptance, how could it be eliminated. The culture of the consumers defines the way the brand would be accepted in the unexplored market. To develop the emotional connect with the brand understanding the culture of the consumer is essential to influence and tap the market.

Culture as branding strategy is not only limited to brand but also to the culture of the organization. Your company culture should align with the brand to enhance performance and customer engagement. The health of the customer services is directly proportional to the internal culture of your business. Hence to brief it all, culture is one of the essential medium of communication for your brand. The emotional connection a brand creates through brand engagement with its consumer making it part of their ground-level conversations showcases what culture your brand is spreading.

In short, I believe that focusing on ethos for your brand means one can focus on the right direction, i.e. towards your customers. Brand with global recognition should be more and more influenced by cultural preferences and differences for better customer engagement. However, one must be cautious not to mix religion with business even though religion is part of cultural attributes, so as to promote equality. Business not only should market through local languages, but cultural awareness should be an aspect of your brand customer experience strategy.

Willing to make your brand global, start by making it local first!!

It is also often said that your culture is your brand, and this is true, culture doesn't just affect the internal structures of your organization it also affects all the external aspects too, in particular, your customers. The impact that your culture has on client relationships is dramatic and can go one way or the other, either creating an excellent reputation or an awful one. For a company to achieve a steady, high-quality culture, they need to understand the balance between company success and the personal growth of those in and around it.

To make your brand stand out from the rest, you need to create and maintain exceptional relationships between your employees and your customers, portraying an image of good quality culture within your firm and providing a relatable brand for all potential market sectors. No brand can be unique, distinctive and thriving within the marketplace unless they are special, distinctive and successful within the workplace.

TAKE A LOOK AT THE BELOW FACTS, HOW TO IMPROVE YOUR CULTURE WHICH WILL ALSO HELP YOU BUILD YOUR BRAND:

Define the Culture Internally

Without strictly defining your culture internally, current and new employees will have no idea how to behave and no idea what is truly expected of them regarding their role in the business development. Have a mission statement and policy which all employees must read and abide by and ensure that it covers caring for the customer. Teach your employees to be brilliant with customers, new and old, and watch how your brand improves and transforms. Your brand can only grow if the internal parts of your company grow and so start from the inside out with your plan for increasing brand engagement and awareness.

Tell Your Story

Remember not to do this in a gloating and self-centered kind of way but tell your story subtly and express how you feel about the importance of culture within your organization. Customers will be more engaged with a brand that is seen to treat its employees with compassion and respect. Putting your story out there either using social media, blog posts or news articles can not only get your logo and name into the public eye creating brand visibility, but it can also allow customers to see how you work internally and begin to trust you as a consistent and thoughtful company.

Be Consistent

Remember that consistency is key. Stick to your definition of culture, every day. Don't just be culture aware for one week and hope that will be enough to define your brand and create a solid reputation; you must continue this every day throughout the lifecycle of your brand. Happy employees mean productive working and satisfied customers. Stick to your word, don't break promises to your employees or your clients, and your brand will grow reliably and securely, encouraging more and more customers to experience your products and services.

Encourage Others

One way that businesses can promote themselves without doing so annoyingly and desperately is simply to help others. It is a common known pattern in life that by helping others we can help ourselves, and this applies to the business world as well. Help other businesses to improve their culture and assist them in marketing by promoting their services. This way you will be recognized as a supportive and selfless brand, showing the customer that you have the ability to care for others and so you will care for them.

Relate to the Audience

Perhaps most importantly, you need to make sure your culture relates to your audience. Consider who you want to engage with and then create your culture based on their needs, learn what that particular market sector regard as a high-quality culture, learn what they respect and admire, and develop your business to reflect their views. If you can't relate to your audience, then they won't be able to relate to you, and no brand engagement will occur.

In conclusion, your culture is your brand, and your brand is your culture. Remember to regularly assess the effectiveness of your internal communication and structure, to ensure that you are giving off the correct messages to the potential customers.

11

HUMANIST BRANDING

When it comes to branding these days, many companies are becoming more consumer focused and are putting a lot more time and resources into finding out exactly what the customer desires. Your brand is what makes you stand out from the rest of the competition and helps you to become more memorable in the customers minds, so by relating to them directly and making them feel special, you have a much better chance of growing your client database and retaining current customers, leading to a profitable business.

Branding does not just relate to your logo or image, it relates to your employees, your clients, your customers, your premises, your attitude and most of all your morals. The true identity of your business stems from the internal structure and continues to spread outwards into the marketing and consumer world, creating your brand.

So, let's start with the employees, humanistic branding involves taking great care of your employees, considering their needs, identifying their efforts and hard work, and making them feel safe and valued within their workplace. There are many companies now that involve employee's families in their working life, either by hosting 'bring your child to work' days, arranging events and parties for spouses to attend and even running competitions where by employees can win and earn treats that will also benefit their families such as holidays. Google is one particular company that is highly known to treat their employees with an excellent standard of respect and care. Google offers a friendly, relaxed and safe environment to work in, where employees can bring their loved ones to the office to experience the technology and atmosphere, and they can also work flexible hours in comfortable modern offices. Workplaces like this create a very happy workforce who don't dread coming to work, and so they improve productivity and attendance by sustaining a pleasant environment.

Your customers come next in the priority line after the employees. Without customers, there would be no sales, and without sales, there would be no business. Keeping your customers happy is one thing, but it is even more worthwhile to take that extra step forward and really try to personalize their experience. If a customer feels valued and understood, they are more likely to admire and respect your brand, and therefore they will come back for more services or products in the future. Many companies are now taking that step into focusing heavily on their customers by putting a heavy emphasis on the idea of feedback and reviews. Many restaurants and retailers now reward customers with gifts or free food and drinks, in return for the customer completing a small review or survey about their experience. This not only provides a company with valuable information about the customer's opinion, but it also offers a chance to treat your customer to something nice and show them that you care about them so much that you're willing to offer free goods and services just in return for their highly valued opinion. This is another way to retain customers too as they will like to come back and claim their free items, so you are more likely to see them again soon.

Customer service is one of the most talked about issues concerning various brands, and without good customer service reviews, customers will not trust you or rely on you to provide them with a pleasant experience. It is so important to think about what your customers need regarding customer service; do they need a 24-hour response? Or do they need online or email options rather than just a phone number and call center. Is it possible to offer customer service within your store? Look at how Apple is highly respected for their customer service, the Genius Bar within each apple store offers on the spot problem rectification and lets the brand show them direct care and attention, whilst sorting out their problem for them at that moment right in front of them. Offering the customer, a more personalized and close experience like this is highly regarded and adds a much more human element to the business.

Environmentally friendly businesses are definitely up and coming in today's modern corporate world. Human now has started worrying a lot about the environment for many different reasons and in many different ways. Whether it's to do with global warming, animal testing, or energy wastage and consumption, people love a brand who respects these issues and a brand which are willing to try and make an impact on these worldly problems by influencing a broad range of other businesses and consumers. Many cosmetics are now making sure to list 'not tested on animals' on their products to make sure that consumers know that they care about animals and care about moral issues surrounding animal testing, consumers are also proven to be more likely to buy from these brands as they feel that they have some common morals. Many big brands are removing their leather goods for sale and refusing to use animal skins to manufacture their products, despite the fact that there is still demand and they could make a lot of profit out of these goods. They are choosing to respect the view of the majority of people and relate to them by agreeing with their views and prompting those morals.

Celebrities are personal brands, and they are also a large part of promoting brand awareness as brands will use them for advertising to boost brand engagement. You may notice that many celebrities who use animal fur for fashion are now being shunned by fans on social media, leading to more high-profile celebrities promoting their opposite views and supporting animal safety. Celebrities themselves are trying to become more human and this in turn influences the brands which they represent to become more human alongside them.

Many brands are also now focusing on charity. Charity is a perfect way for brands to become more human as they are relating to the less fortunate and trying to help the underprivileged, which always warms the heart of the consumer and relates to common feelings and thoughts. Brands such as Toms which make footwear, have an initiative whereby if a customer buys a pair of shoes, they will provide a free pair of shoes to a child in a third world country. This not only shows the customer that they care about this cause, but it also encourages the customer to buy from them and help them to support the less fortunate.

Your business is the environment in which your brand exists, and the structure, internal climate and culture demonstrate to outsiders the foundation upon which your company has been built. Within your workplace what the employees experience defines your brand, and employees soak up every vibe within the atmosphere, and in turn, they pass this on to your customers through their attitude, interactions, decisions and choices during their working life. The products and services which you supply are truly a big part of your brand, but even bigger than that is the relationships that you have with others and the value you place upon these relationships. As an employer or leader, it is crucial to ensure that your employees are happy and therefore are providing your customers with an excellent brand experience, leaving them with a great impression of what you are all about. The customers highest measure of trust is based upon how consistent the quality of the customer service is that they receive from you. Every time they interact with you, whether positive or negative, they are interacting with your brand and creating an opinion of you in their brains, so it is paramount to ensure that the lasting impression they get is of committed and caring service. Many brands are failing or getting bad reputations due to customers receiving bad experiences due to unhappy staff in the workplace, and this shows us that the branding morals must start internally and need to be expelled outwards creating a high-quality tree of service for all involved.

No matter how small one employee may seem, it is vital that you show them that they are part of something much bigger, and their individual experience and attitude really does count and make a difference within the organization. Employees must be treated as humans and not as numbers with specific roles, it is so helpful to involve them in decision making and respect their opinions no matter how irrelevant you deem it to be. By making your internal structure feel like individually valued humans, you have a much better chance of them passing this on to the externals in terms of customers and clients. Treat them how you'd like them to treat your customers.

Trust is one of the most important aspects of human relationships and one of the most valued traits within any human personality, and so brands are now focusing more on this human element of life to ensure that customers have a trusting relationship with them encouraging commitment and long-lasting interactions, just as it would in a romantic relationship or friendship for humans themselves.

Trust is absolutely utmost to maintaining your customers, and so you must make that your brand values. Your marketing messages should be fully aligned internally before promoting them to the world because no trust in the workplace drains productivity and eventually creates losses for the brand.

Hiring the right people is crucial, many workers these days care nothing for the brand or customers and simply want the money at the end of the month, but these humans are not going to create a great image for you in terms of enthusiasm and care. Promote your brand as a brand that is not hierarchy based but is founded upon a team of individually respected humans who are all working together towards the same cause; making customers happy. By promoting your brand like this, you will drive brand engagement and attract the best internal structure for the job and therefore have a better chance of creating humanistic awareness for your brand.

In conclusion, branding that is not humanized, will not relate to drive brand engagement. Without carefully considering the needs and desires of the humans you are trying to appeal to, you will have no chance of creating or enhancing your relationship with them. Brands must consider their relationships with customers, as a husband would with a wife, or a mother and a child, and think carefully about the others feelings. Your whole business profits and life cycle depends on your brand awareness and reputation, so it is fully worthwhile to focus all your thoughts and resources into making sure you are sending out the best message and impression possible.

12

NETWORKING

There are many tactics and tools that we can use to help a brand grow its awareness and credibility, but one of the most beneficial ways of doing this is by creating solid links and relationships with other influential and experienced business leaders, and committed clients. Having good business relationships and finding reliable and successful partners to team up with is crucial to the progression of any brand. There are many ways in which networking can happen, and a lot of this is done online using the internet and social media. However, there is something more special and personal about doing this activity face to face rather than from behind a computer screen.

But, what is networking?

Networking is a socioeconomic business activity by which businesspeople engage to form business connections and to identify, create, or act upon business opportunities, share information and seek potential partners for growth.

Forbes conducted the study on the importance of face-to-face networking, and it is unbelievable that 84% of the respondents said that they prefer face-to-face meetings if it comes to building business connections.

When questioned why they preferred in-person business meetings, here are some of their responses:

- 75% respondents prefer it due to the prospect of more social interactions and bonding

- 77% liked the ability to understand facial expressions and body language during in-person meetings

- 85% of respondents believes it builds stronger and meaningful relationships

The data is overwhelming and is in complete support of face-to-face business networking. Social Media is probably the best way to spread brand awareness and influence the buyers but if you are looking to focus on business to business networking or expanding your business than social media alone is not enough.

If you want to learn a bit more about offline networking strategies, then continue reading and enlighten yourself as to how leaders can mingle in real life to increase awareness and engagement for their brand.

NETWORKING EVENTS

Networking events are becoming increasingly popular in many fields of work, whether this be sales, medical related, law firms, restaurants, hospitality or more. It is often that business leaders and higher-level employees are invited to events where they can enjoy good food-drink and socialize with other like-minded business entrepreneurs for the purpose of getting their brand name out there and learning expert skills relating to how other businesses promote their brands.

Networking events give the chance to gain an insight into the way other brands work and offer an opportunity to be inspired while listening to the stories and success stories of others, whilst also sharing your own experience and therefore making others aware of who you are and what your brand is all about. Establishing relationships like this is proven to create long-lasting interactions from one brand to another and allows managers and entrepreneurs to get to know each other on a more personal level. After all, a smiling and enthusiastic face is far more memorable than an online username.

The way you act and behave will directly affect the reputation of your brand, so this is a chance to use your human personality traits and qualities to portray the right image for your brand. Always aim to go in there with an open mind, listening carefully to others and also carefully and considerately sharing viewpoints and taking opportunities to raise awareness of your brand.

SOCIAL CLUBS

Social Clubs are another ideal location to meet other business-minded individuals and promote awareness and brand engagement opportunities for your brand. Some clubs will even allow you to do some small free of charge marketing by leaving leaflets in their premises or maybe putting an advert or your logo in their front window or other location where it can catch the eyes of others.

Most importantly, if you are enjoying a sport or hobby and you meet another person there, then you are likely to have something in common already, your love for the game. An example of this is using golf clubs. Golf is a sport known to attract many business individuals, and it also includes many social aspects before and after the game, as the clubs usually provide right premises to have a drink or something to eat. Finding a golfing partner or group can give the opportunity to calmly play the game you love, spending hours conversing and sharing thoughts with other people. This is an excellent opportunity to share your brand ideas, promote the objectives and ethos of your brand and hopefully gain either new clients and customers or new business relationships through which you can assist each other with brand promotion and reputation. Teaming up with a business that is already of an established brand name and has a great reputation and following, can be a game changer for many companies and can give them a real boost up the ladder in terms of competition and business success. Golf clubs are also notorious for arranging business networking events and special gala dinners for golf club members, meaning that you will get chance to meet others who love the game and love business, again giving more chance to discuss your brand, discuss their brand and hopefully then watch a great corporate relationship blossom.

CONTINUING EDUCATION

Further Education is another excellent opportunity not only to take the chance to develop your personal growth but also to meet others who have the same aims and interests. Showing enthusiasm to better yourself gives a great impression to customers, clients and business partners as they can truly believe that you are putting your all into your brand and are determined and focused on being successful no matter how hard you have to work.

Continuing education and professional development are essential ingredients for successful brands. In this ever-changing world, there are many factors that drive the need for continuing education for entrepreneurs: abundant access to knowledge, constant technology changes, extended global interactions, shifts in the industry, and increasing entry-level skills and requirements. To be successful in your field having an ongoing education is a minimum requirement. Since knowledge and information are growing every day, your education must also increase to keep up.

Within further education, whether this is at a university, college or privately-run development institute, you are likely to learn so much about the topic which you have chosen to study. You can then apply what learn to your business strategy plan enabling you to give your brand a well-educated and knowledgeable basis to grow on. While studying you can likely find others who have the same goals as you and can then assist each other to achieve your goals, either by working together to progress one brand, or by supporting each other with your separate business brands, either way, a problem shared is a problem halved and supporting each other is absolutely supreme in growing successfully as an individual and brand.

WORKSHOPS AND SEMINARS

Workshops and Seminars is another way through which you can drive brand engagement and encourage people to come and find out what your brand is all about, promoting your morals and ethos while drawing clients in and retaining current customers.

As an entrepreneur, you've probably have spent years building a reputation as an expert in your field. Whether you're a successful entrepreneur or in early years of your career you surely have something to share with your customers and audience on how they can benefit from using your brand.

A workshop or seminar is one of the most powerful tools you can use to showcase expertise, build credibility and establish yourself as an expert in your industry. At the same moment, you're generating exposure for yourself, forming new relationships and eventually growing your business.

LINKEDIN

LinkedIn, although not strictly falling into the category of offline networking but can be an ideal hub where you can look around the local area for other professionals with the same interests and ideas. Use this contact portal to find and invite suitable people to your networking events, seminars and workshops.

Hubspot conducted a reach study and found that LinkedIn referral traffic had the highest visitor-to-lead conversion rate as a comparison to any other social networking platform; higher than Facebook or Twitter. They discovered that LinkedIn had average conversion rates of 2.74%, compared to Twitter's .69% and Facebook's .77%.

LinkedIn can be true game changer for business to business

companies. This is a brilliant platform for getting a brief history of what other people are all about, showing you their education, work experience, knowledge, extra skills and interests, mean that when you do meet up with these people, you have a lot to talk about and you can converse with them on their level, exploring more about their interests and engaging with their expertise. LinkedIn is also a great way to prepare yourself if you are attending an event or holding a workshop and have an idea of what names are going to be there, as you can research them in advance, so you know who exactly you are dealing with.

GUEST SPEAKER

Guest speaking opportunities don't come up too often, but if you can achieve such role, it can create immense awareness and promotion of your brand. Give students, viewers, clients, or customers the chance to engage directly with you (the face behind the brand), this makes the brand appear and feel more human and thus much more reliable and relatable.

Guest speakers are often invited in universities and educational institutions for the purpose of education, look at local educational establishments which run business related courses and offer to go in and talk to the students about various business topics and your brand itself. This is a great chance to offer some free merchandise in the form of pens, keyrings, magnets etc. which allows you to keep your logo fresh in the mind of the recipient. Speaking also gives you the chance to show the listeners the personality behind the brand, allowing them to relate and empathise with what you are all about and therefore creating more engagement at a higher level.

BUSINESS CARDS

Business cards sound like an obvious tactic, but it's surprising how many new businesses do not make use of business cards and rely wholly on online advertising and promotion. But using business cards for networking is more prominent than ever since clients are craving a personal touch when it comes to working with a brand. So it is ideal to share business cards and swap them with other entrepreneurs, allowing the chance to retain details and converse in the future to help each other and developing reliable and trustworthy business relationships that add to the profitability of all brands involved.

I strongly believe the business card is valuable for start of the conversation with new people or potential clients, so it is important to have a very impressive business card and some rules must be followed to create the first great impression of your personal brand and business brand through a business card.

Keep following points in your mind while creating business cards:

Who, What, Where, Why - Try putting all these information and

- Make it easily readable
- Use QR Code
- Use brand logo
- Keep it align with your business theme
- Use ecofriendly paper

Below are some basic rules to follow for the powerful and productive exchange of business cards:

Always carry your cards and plenty of them. There is nothing more unprofessional to say, "Oh, I'm sorry. I just gave out my last card." or " I'm sorry, I forgot my cards.

Keep your business cards in card case that protects them from wear and tear, and keeps them crisp and fresh. There could be nothing more unprofessional than dirty business cards.

Don't Search for your business card; it looks shabby and unorganized when someone has to go through every pant and coat pocket or briefcase to search business cards.

Give and take cards with your right hand; this makes a vast difference when doing business globally.

Keep the other person's card respectfully; casual approach can hurt the card giver.

Give the card straight, so the person who is holding it can see it without turning it around.

Comment about a card when you take it. Note logo, business name, tagline, qualification or some other information. Your one good positive comment can start the conversation and can create a great impression.

Keep your card updated, if your contact information changes make sure you print new updated card don't handwrite.

In conclusion, there are many ways in which networking can be carried out, but sadly in the modern-day world, people are entirely reliant on the internet which does take the humanist side and personalisation away from the process of doing business. Face to face interactions must not be disregarded and are invaluable when it comes to really knowing another human being. Making use of all the suggested networking ideas is a great way to raise awareness for your brand and yourself as an individual, which in essence impacts directly on your business success in the long run. Face to Face networking should be equally practised along with your digital marketing and promotion. Always remember that just because there are new ways of doing things, this does not mean that old methods are now deemed useless, and it is advised to keep a balance of traditional and modern strategies mixed within your business development plan in order to really get the most out of the current market situation and give your business the best chance of flourishing in to a sustainable and profitable brand.

THINK SECTION

THINK AND WRITE DOWN YOUR PLANS AND THOUGHTS

THINK SECTION

THINK AND WRITE DOWN YOUR PLANS AND THOUGHTS

THINK SECTION

THINK AND WRITE DOWN YOUR PLANS AND THOUGHTS

THINK SECTION

THINK AND WRITE DOWN YOUR PLANS AND THOUGHTS

*A brand is no longer what we tell the customers.
It is what customers tell each other.*

GAURAV GULATI

Made in United States
North Haven, CT
21 January 2024